A CHRONICLE OF IRISH SAINTS

A
CHRONICLE
OF
IRISH SAINTS

LAURENCE FLANAGAN

THE
BLACKSTAFF
PRESS

BELFAST

First published in 1990 by
The Blackstaff Press Limited
3 Galway Park, Dundonald, Belfast BT16 0AN, Northern Ireland

Text editor Éilis Brennan
Typeset by Textflow Services Limited
Printed by The Bath Press

British Library Cataloguing in Publication Data
Flanagan, Laurence
A chronicle of Irish saints.
1. Ireland. Saints – Biographies – Collections
I. Title
274.15
ISBN 0-85640-436-5

TO MY DAUGHTERS
GRÁINNE CAOIMHE DEIRDRE,
DUNLA BRONACH FIONNUALA
AND LAOISE CAITRÍONA BRÍDÍN

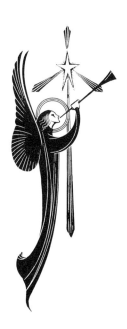

CONTENTS

MAP OF IRELAND
SHOWING PLACES ASSOCIATED
WITH SOME OF
THE IRISH SAINTS

INTRODUCTION

This book has no pretensions to being a major work of innovative scholarship. It is, rather, intended to introduce to the general reader the wealth of Early Christian Ireland, not only in the form of the sadly under-used names of native Irish saints, or the tales that have been woven around them, but also in the visual wealth of the remains of churches, of metalwork, of manuscripts and literature which form part of our heritage.

To these are added the local veneration – still persisting in this day and age – of local saints. My own children, as tokens of their participation in their heritage, bear the names of local (to us) saints: Caoimhe of Killinchy, Co. Down; Bronach of Kilbroney, Co. Down, and Caitríona, for Catherine of Killybegs, Co. Donegal.

In addition to the brief biographical notes of some hundred Irish saints, assembled from a variety of sources, there is the Calendar of Irish Saints, again selected from a variety of sources, but mainly, inevitably, the extant martyrologies or calendars of Irish saints, to provide a selection of names from which prospective parents can make their choice. No guide to pronunciation is given: differences of dialect throughout Ireland, as evidenced by the difference in pronunciation of the simple Sean between South and North, make such a guide both dangerous and impracticable. The best advice to any potential, non-Irish-speaking user is to seek out, in his or her area, a person aware of local pronunciations of Irish names.

St Patrick (Richard King,
Capuchin Annual)

THE EARLY CHRISTIAN CHURCH IN IRELAND

A bishop of the Early Irish Church,
bearing bell and crozier, on a stone at
Killadeas, Co. Fermanagh (Historic
Monuments Branch, Department of
Environment for Northern Ireland)

The introduction of Christianity to Ireland is traditionally attributed to St Patrick. There were, however, Christian missionaries in Ireland before the arrival of Patrick. For example, there was Palladius, sent from Rome in 431 to 'the Irish who believed in Christ', but of whose activities there is little record. There was Ibhar, who is supposed to have established a pre-Patrician church on Beggerin Island [*Beag Éire*, Little Ireland] near Wexford. There is little doubt, however, that Patrick, whose arrival in Ireland is dated, at the earliest, to 432, was the person responsible for the spread and rooting of Christianity throughout the country. He is credited with establishing some sixty churches, with bishops, in the course of his mission, mainly in the North.

While Patrick talks of the sons of the Irish and the daughters of their kings, who became 'monks and virgins in Christ', it appears that the Patrician Church was not, in essence, monastic, though even the earliest may have had residential accommodation. The Church in Ireland did, however, fairly rapidly become monastic, with communities of monks, or nuns, being established, with abbots and abbesses in charge. During the sixth and seventh centuries monasticism expanded throughout Ireland. Many of the new monasteries were founded by monks who are said to have been trained at Candida Casa at Whithorn in Galloway, Scotland.

Many of the Irish monasteries developed schools, which became important centres of learning and attracted to them the foremost scholars of their day. Some monks, in their desire to worship God, sought seclusion from the world and established smaller monasteries, or hermitages, in remote places, such as the islands off the west coast. Others felt the need to share their faith in God and left Ireland to go abroad as missionaries and to found monasteries. This brought the Irish Church into greater contact, and often conflict, with the Church in mainland Europe, and Rome.

As the monasteries grew in importance and wealth through the eighth century – some of them were more like small cities – they increasingly attracted the interest and interference of secular power. To combat this secular interference the reform movement, known as the *Céile Dé*, or Culdee, grew up, with its emphasis on anchoritic asceticism and rather puritanical idealism.

Towards the end of the eighth century the monasteries also attracted the attention of the marauding bands of Vikings – first the remote islands, then the wealthier foundations on the mainland – and were attacked by them. Many were totally destroyed and even abandoned, though others were rebuilt. A slight respite from the destruction was gained in 1014 with the defeat of the Norse, or Vikings, by Brian Boru.

The Synod of Rathbreasail in 1111 was responsible for reorganising the structure of the Irish Church. A proper diocesan system, with officially designated cathedrals, was adopted. Some of the earlier monastic foundations were chosen as the centres of sees and others were not. The reorganisation of the Irish monasteries and the introduction to Ireland of continental orders was the brain-child of St Malachy, by dint of his association with St Bernard of Clairvaux.

The first two orders to be introduced to Ireland under the influence of Malachy were the Cistercians, whose first Irish house was at Mellifont, in 1142, and the Arroasians, or Augustinians. The Church in Ireland was coming into line with western Christendom.

Mermaid from the *Book of Kells*

Oratory of Gallarus, Co. Kerry
(Commissioners of Public Works
in Ireland)

CHURCH BUILDINGS

Church at St John's Point, Co. Down
(Historic Monuments Branch,
Department of Environment for
Northern Ireland)

Temple MacDuagh, Inishmore, Aran
Islands, Co. Galway

The earliest church buildings in Ireland were pretty certainly constructed of wood, consequently none has survived, though traces of wooden structures have been recorded under stone churches. However, examples of later small stone-built churches, which preserve structural features of their wooden predecessors, do survive. Such churches, with their side-walls projecting beyond the gable, to form what are called antae, are not uncommon. Examples are Temple MacDuagh on the Aran Island of Inishmore, Co. Galway, and the church at St John's Point in Co. Down.

Sometimes the copying of a wooden prototype is recalled even more strongly by the presence of a sort of Y-shaped finial, suggesting the crossing of beams supporting the roof. Representation of what, apparently, are wooden churches appear, moreover, in the *Book of Kells* and as the finial of Muiredach's Cross at Monasterboice in Co. Louth.

That churches built entirely of stone existed, but were rare, is suggested by the name of Duleek [*daimh liag*, house of stones or stone church] in Co. Meath. The many stone-roofed churches, surviving especially in the west of Ireland, such as the church on St MacDara's Island in Co. Galway, or the corbel-built structure known as the Oratory of Gallarus in Co. Kerry, clearly owe nothing directly to wooden prototypes.

The most striking feature of these surviving churches is their size. Sometimes they are less that two metres by three metres. Even when they were incorporated in monastic settlements they were seldom very large: instead of building much larger churches, the tendency seemed to be to build more and more small ones. Larger churches did, however, exist. There is something domestic, rather than public, about their scale and, in some ways, they are reminiscent of the community's being often referred to as the 'family' or *muintir*.

While many of the early churches are plain and unadorned, often simple rectangular boxes, descriptions in documents suggest that the larger and, presumably, more important were quite lavishly decorated inside. The adoption of 'Irish Romanesque' architecture led to the presence of elaborately decorated doorways, with curved arches in place of the simple trabeate form with a large stone or lintel surmounting typically Irish inclined jambs.

On monastic sites the church was often accompanied by dwelling-places, such as Nendrum in Co. Down, where they appear to have been thatched wood-built structures, perhaps with a stone foundation-course. In later times, maybe as a response to the Viking raids, the Round Tower appeared on monastic sites to serve as a combined belfry, which is what their Irish name *cloigtheach* [bell house] suggests as having been their primary function, or a watch-tower, because they often have windows at the top, commanding views in all four directions, or a place of refuge, since their entrances are almost universally on the first floor and accessed by ladder, or a strongroom for monastic valuables, because the destruction of a Round Tower and treasures is often reported. Although to an extent self-defeating from the security point of view, it is an indication, in the relatively trackless wastes of early Ireland, that here was the monastery. Remains of buildings, possibly used as workshops or scriptoria or libraries, are extremely rare, though possibly traces of one such building were discovered at Nendrum in Co. Down.

Slate from Nendrum, Co. Down, used as a 'sketch-pad' for lettering

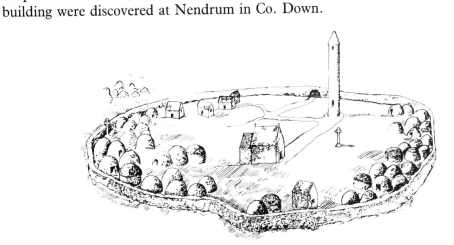

Conjectural reconstruction of the monastic enclosure at Kells, Co. Meath

5

A panel from the *Book of Durrow*

High Cross at Ahenny, Co. Tipperary
(Commissioners of Public Works
in Ireland)

ART

The most obvious artistic achievement of the Irish monasteries was in stone-carving, not only as an embellishment of the church itself, but also in the form, first of the early grave-slabs, often decorated with crosses of greater or lesser complexity, and then of the free-standing cross-slabs, of which the most splendid example is at Fahan in Co. Donegal, and finally of High Crosses – as much a symbol of Early Christian Ireland as the Round Tower. These are to be seen all over the country: at Arboe, Co. Tyrone, at Monasterboice, Co. Louth, at Clonmacnoise, Co. Offaly, at Moone, Co. Kildare. Most of them bear scriptural scenes, often from the Old Testament on one side and from the New Testament on the other, presumably to serve as a sort of visual aid for teaching purposes.

The art practised in the monasteries was not confined to stone-carving, however. In the scriptoria Gospel-manuscripts, often quite beautifully illuminated, like those of the *Book of Kells* and the *Book of Durrow*, were produced. Metal-working was carried on in the workshops, creating, for church use, such masterpieces as the Ardagh Chalice, the Cross of Cong, as well as the simple bronze bells that were such typical accessories of Irish ecclesiastics. Here too were produced the elaborate shrines, be it for the staves of early saints, like the Crozier of St Davnet, or pieces of their bodies, such as the Shrine of St Lachtin's Arm, or Gospel books, like the Shrine of Dimma's Book, that form such a major and spectacular part of Irish ecclesiastical art.

Silver chalice from Ardagh,
Co. Tipperary (National Museum
of Ireland)

The shrine known as Breac Maodhog
(National Museum of Ireland)

RELIQUARIES AND SHRINES

The enshrining of such items as saints' staves, arms and books was a regular procedure in the Early Irish Church, which continued even after the reforms of St Malachy. Apart from the obvious motive of devotion to the saint in question, such relics were thought to be endowed with special powers.

Fiacre is reported to have administered the Last Sacrament to the dying Comgal of Bangor, and then to have brought back his embalmed arm to Ullard as a relic.

Very special – and often costly – shrines were created for these relics. They were carried into battle and, occasionally, as happened in 1178 when John de Courcy attacked Downpatrick, were lost as a result. The most precious of all, St Patrick's Crozier, the Staff of Jesus [*Bachall Íosa*], was burned in Dublin in 1538.

A crozier – the badge of office of a Bishop of the Early Irish Church (National Museum of Ireland)

Shrine of St Laichtin's Arm, from the monastery of Donoughmore, Co. Cork (National Museum of Ireland)

7

LITERATURE

The range of literary effort to which the monks in early Irish monasteries devoted themselves was prodigious. Apart from studies of the scriptures, which were used not only in Ireland, but on the continent as well – often plagiaristically ascribed to better known continental authorities – one field of study which developed was historical writing.

Annals, year-by-year accounts of what had happened, with the earlier parts tending to be pseudo-historical rather than factually historical, were compiled at many monasteries, copies of which, despite the destruction of monastic libraries, have survived, such as the *Annals of Inisfallen* and the *Annals of Clonmacnoise*. Saints' 'Lives' and martyrologies were compiled. The *Martyrology of Aengus* is one example, which is, quite simply, a list of saints, foreign and Irish, arranged under the days of the year, but in verse. Like the others it 'turns a virgin into a man, invents saints out of a place-name'.

The earliest example in prose is the *Martyrology of Tallaght*. A typical entry in this, for 1 February, albeit described as 'The Kalends of February', reads in Latin:

Dormitatio sanctae Brigitae lxx anno aetatis suae. Derlugach. Beonni virginis. Cinni sac. Airennan moccu Foduibh

A scribe pictured in the *Book of Kells*

meaning that on this date is recorded: The falling asleep of Saint Bridget in the seventieth year of her life. The Feasts of Derlugach, Beonna, a virgin, Cinne, a priest, Airennan, descendant of Fodub.

The majority of the 'Lives' contain little genuine information about the saints, with some honourable exceptions, but they reveal attitudes to them on the part of later generations of writers. Two conclusions seem inescapable: that leprosy was rampant in Early Christian Ireland, as reflected, indeed, in place names, such as Leopardstown, where the exotic leopard seems less likely than the undesired leper, and that most writers of saints' 'Lives', commencing in January, became less enthusiastic as the year progressed.

In addition to such church-related literature, the monks copied down the pagan literature of the country: we owe the preservation of the stories of the

Ulster Cycle, with its tales of Cuchulain, to the endeavours of Irish monks. They also composed poetry and some of it was very fine indeed.

SAINTS AND THEIR NAMES

There are literally hundreds of Irish saints. Some achieved their status by being especially learned, some – remarkably few – by martyrdom, some by their noteworthy service to God and the Church, some, it would seem, simply from being in the right place at the right time. Interestingly, however, only three have been actually canonised: Malachy, in 1190, by Clement III, Laurence O'Toole, *c.* 1220, by Honorius III, and Oliver Plunkett, in 1975, by Paul VI.

There are many with the same name, which causes a great deal of confusion. It is understandable that some names of certain saints should be used again and again, as a mark of respect and, possibly, in an attempt to have a share in the sanctity of its original owner. Records, which are even nearly contemporary with the events, are sparse, and often a single, not certainly identifying, name is used. Some, on the other hand, have a multiplicity of names.

It has been demonstrated, for example, that Colman of Dromore was also known as Colum, Mocholmoc, Mochonne, Dochonna, Mochumma – some of which are easily explained legitimate linguistic variations. They do, however, give rise to a further extension of the list of names ascribed to this single saint: we next have a series containing Cummae, Cuimme, Commae, Coimme, Caimme, as well as Cummoc, Cammoc, Comman, Camman, Cuimmin, Cuimmine, Caimmin, Caimmine. When to these lists are added Conna or Connae they overlap confusingly with both Colum, as Colm Cille, which is the same as Columba, and Cainnech [Canice of Kilkenny], with the addition of Latin and English forms of names of Irish saints, such as the Latin Columba [dove], for Colm or Colum, which also means dove. Or the English Kevin for one of the Irish spellings of the saint of Glendalough – Caoimhín – gives a very wide choice of forms or spellings, as well as contributing to a general and widespread confusion.

While some saints have no known feast day, others appear to have more than one. And some saints are more positively identified by the use of their

Initials from the *Book of Kells* (Trinity College Dublin)

patronymic, being the name of a father, grandfather or other male ancestor, or a gloss on the area where they were born or with which they were associated, others are not.

Sometimes the acts of one saint are absorbed into the life of another, particularly easily where the names are the same or have variants in common. Among others, the prefixing of terms like 'Mo-', which has an affectionate, more or less diminutive 'dear little', effect, in such attested examples as Mo-Laisse, Mo-Cholmoc, was common.

PLACE NAMES

Certain Irish words are used specifically of churches. The word *domhnach* is one example, apparently used particularly in the early days of Patrick's mission to designate a parish church, and often, accordingly, qualified by the name of the district in which it was located, as *Domhnach Mor Mhá Cobha*, Donaghmore [The Great Church] of Magh Cobha in Co. Down.

When the Irish Church became monastic the Irish word *cill* supplanted *domhnach* as the common word for church or monastery, appearing in place names in English as Kil-, which can all too easily be confused with the Irish word *coill*, meaning wood, understandably widespread in Ireland, and also appearing as Kil- in place names.

Cill, or Kil-, is often followed by the name of a saint, like Kilbeggan in Co. Westmeath is Beagan's Church; Kilconnell in Co. Galway is Conall's Church. Other words used are *díseart*, as in Desertmartin, usually meaning a hermitage; *teampall*, as in Templepatrick; and *eaglais*, usually without a qualifier, as in Eglish. Other words which can signify a church include *teach* [house], as in Tedavnet [Davnet's house], *both* [hut], as in Raphoe [fort-hut], *lann*, as in Lambeg [small church]. *Mainistir* [monastery] is another obvious term.

Laurence Flanagan
Belfast, 1990

USERS' GUIDE

NOTE

Saints' names and their variants are used in the calendar sections and index.

Saint A male saint whose feast day is celebrated on that date.

Saint* A female saint whose feast day is celebrated on that date.

SAINT A male saint whose feast day is celebrated on that date and of whom a brief biographical note is given on that date.

SAINT* A female saint whose feast day is celebrated on that date and of whom a brief biographical note is given on that date.

[ ] Square brackets used for short translations of place names, isolated words and variants of saints' names within the text.

ANUARY

1 Airmeadhach; Aodhán; BEOC; BEOG; Brocan; Colman; Comnatan★; Crone; Cuan; DABEOC; Eochaid; Ernab; Fainche★; Fionntán; MOBEOC; Sciath; Tobrea

2 Ainbithen★; Lochaidh; MAINCHÍN; MUINCHIN; MUNCHIN; Scoithin

3 Cillian; Fionnlugh; Fiontann

4 Aodh; Fianait★; Maolam; Mochumma

5 Airendan; Ciar★; Ciarán; Mochumma

6 Curnan; Diarmaid; DIMA; DIMMA; DIOMA; DOMAINGERT; Lassair★; Muadhnait★; Osnat; Tuilelath★

7 Brigh★; Corcan; Cormac; Cronan; Cuircne; Dalua; Donnán; Éimhín; Inna; Modichu; Molacca

8 Cillian; Cuac★; Ercnac★; Fionán; Moliba; Neachtan; Saran

9 Baithin; Breannain; Ciarán; Faolan; Finnia★; Guaire; Siubsech★

10 DERMOT; DIARMAID; Diman; Maolodhran; Toman; Tuilelath★

11 Alten; Amphadan; Beandan; Earnán; EITHNE★; ETHNEA★; Failbhe; FEDELMIA★; FIDELMA★; Orthinis; Ronan; Suibhne

12 Boithin; Conan; Cuimín; Foelan; Laidcenn; Lochein; Sinell

13 Ailill; Colman; Deuraid; Mainchin; Mochonna; Ronan; Saran

14 Beatan; Flann

15 Aitche★; DEIRDRE★; ÍDE★; ITA★; ITE★; MIDA★

16 Cillian; Diarmaid; Lochan; Maeiosa; Monoa★; Ninnidh

17 Earnán; Mica★; Ultan

18 Aedamar★; Ana★

19 Baoithin; Bláth; Blathmac; Fachtna; Suibhne

20 Aonghus; Bhauch; Cronan; Fearghus; FECHIN; FEICHÍN; MO-ECA;
   MO-FHECA

21 Brighis★; Eglionna★; Fainche★; Flann; Saighin

22 Boga; Colma★; Colman; Guaire; Lasair★; Lonán

23 Ceallach; Coinneach; Lucan

24 Buadhan; Guasacht; MANCHAN

25 Aodh; Eochaid; Finche★; Guaire

26 Eirnín

27 Croine; Lucan; Muirgin; Naal

28 Acobhran; Canneire★; Neallan

29 Bláth★; Cronan; Eochaidh

30 Ailbe; Annichad; Cronan; Eanan; Maelbhrighde

31 AODHÁN; Ciarnan; Coinneach; Eabhnat★; Lughaidh; M'AODHOG;
   Maoilanfhaidh; MOEDOC; MOGUE; Siadhal; Sillan

1 January

BEOC [BEOG, MOBEOC, DABEOC]
of Lough Derg, Co. Donegal

St Patrick's Purgatory, Lough Derg,
Co. Donegal

Beoc is said to have been the son of a Welsh prince, Brecan, possibly himself of Irish descent, and a noble British lady, called Marcella, and to have lived in the fifth or sixth century. He is also said to have been the youngest of ten brothers, all of whom, as well as seven sisters, are supposed to have entered the Church.

He came to Ireland and found his way to Lough Derg in Co. Donegal where he established a church, which was to become celebrated as St Patrick's Purgatory, on the largest of the three islands.

One night while he and his monks were conducting a vigil, a wonderful brightness appeared to the north. The rather awestruck monks asked their master what it meant. He replied:

> In that direction, where you have seen the brilliant light, the Lord himself, at a future time, will light a shining lamp which, by its brightness, must miraculously glorify the Church of Christ. This will be Colm, the son of Feidlimid, son of Fergus, and his mother will be Eithne. For learning he will be distinguished; in body and in soul he will be chaste and he will possess the gifts of prophecy.

On Saints' Island on Lough Derg are the ruins of a medieval church which are believed to mark the site of the church founded by Beoc.

2 January

MUNCHIN [MUINCHIN, MAINCHÍN]
of Limerick, Co. Limerick

Church at Mungret, Co. Limerick

Very little is known about Munchin, but he is said to have been the son of a nobleman called Sedna and a nephew of Bloid, King of Thomond. He is credited with founding a church at Mungret on the River Shannon near where the City of Limerick now stands and to have been made a bishop by St Patrick.

According to local tradition the community here contained 1,500 monks, 500 of whom were devoted to preaching, another 500 so organised as to provide a perpetual full choir, performing day and night, while the remaining 500 were old men of exemplary piety who devoted themselves to charitable and religious works. Munchin is the patron of the Diocese of Limerick.

In its heyday it boasted six churches. The site of his monastery is now marked only by the ruins of the thirteenth- to fifteenth-century abbey, a small thirteenth-century oratory and a twelfth-century church with a trabeate – a simple slab as lintel – doorway.

6 January

DIMMA [DIMA, DIOMA, DIMA DUBH, DOMAINGERT]
of Connor, Co. Antrim

Dimma's father was called Aengus and he was born in Munster, a member of the ruling family. When the saint was young he was placed in the monastery of St Colman-Elo, at Lynally in Co. Offaly, who instructed him to partake of generous food to prepare his constitution for the rigorous life he was to undergo.

Church at Lynally, Co. Offaly

This ties in with a story that he was instructed by St Cronan, Abbot of Roscrea in Co. Tipperary, to transcribe for him a Book of Gospels. This Dimma did in forty days, in the course of which he took neither food nor rest. However, this achievement is likely to have been undertaken by another scribe of the same name.

Dimma settled at Connor in Co. Antrim, and later became its bishop. He died on 6 January 658.

A Gospel Book, encased in an elaborate shrine, known as 'Dimma's Book and Shrine', originally in the monastery of Roscrea, is now preserved in the Library of Trinity College, Dublin.

10 January

DERMOT [DIARMAID OF INCHCLERAUN (INIS CLOTHRANN)]
of Lough Ree, Co. Longford

Dermot was born in Connacht, of high birth on both his father's and his mother's side. In his pursuit of solitude he sought out a lonely island on Lough Ree, often inaccessible by open boat when storms curl over the waters, where, in 540, he founded his monastery.

St Dermot with St Columba
(Robert Gibbings)

He is renowned as teacher and confessor to Kieran of Clonmacoise. Even in the nineteenth century boatmen on the lough claimed to have seen him – 'a tall and stately figure', walking from Inchcleraun along the waves.

There are fairly extensive ruins of the monastic site, the oldest being, appropriately, *Teampall Diarmada* [Dermot's Church], a small oratory. There are four other churches and remains of conventual buildings. A beautiful ivory statue of Dermot was formerly preserved on the island. It was removed for protection in the seventeenth century, but unfortunately it disappeared.

11 January

EITHNE [ETHNEA] *and* FIDELMA [FEDELMIA]
Daughters of King Laoghaire

The stories of Eithne and Fidelma must constitute the strangest – and briefest – lives of any Irish saints. Their father became King of Ireland, with his residence at Tara, Co. Meath, in 428. In 433 Patrick had been invited to attend the court of Laoghaire. Preceded by the Crucifix and accompanied by his clerics, the saint made a solemn and dignified approach to the gates of the palace, which flew open.

Then ensued the famous contest between the saint and the Wizard Lucamael, which resulted in the death of Lucamael and some of those who sought to take revenge for his death by attacking Patrick. It also led to the instant conversion and baptism of the survivors.

The two daughters of Laoghaire, Eithne the Fair and Fidelma the Rosy, however, were not present at their father's court during these events. Their encounter with Patrick, therefore, as he was making his way to Croghan, the residence of the kings of Connacht, came as a surprise to them. Awestruck by the unfamiliar appearance of the saint and his clerics, they questioned him about what he was and where he came from. Patrick instructed them at length in the Christian faith. The two young women were filled with enthusiasm and ardour and cried out: 'What you desire us to do, we shall willingly perform.' Patrick promptly baptised them. No sooner had he done so than they desired to take the veil. They then entreated him to free them from the prison of their bodies, so that they might indeed behold the Lord. Their wish was speedily

Eithne and Fidelma
(*Irish Catholic Directory*)

granted and, lying together in the one bed, they 'quitted their earthly tabernacle and went to meet their Heavenly Spouse, sweetly falling asleep in the Lord'.

Their kinfolk and friends lamented them sorrowfully for three days and then buried them. On the place where they were buried a church was erected. Later their remains were translated to Armagh.

St Ita's Church, Killeedy, Co. Limerick

15 January

ITA [ITE, ÍDE, MIDA, DEIRDRE]
of Killeedy, Co. Limerick

St Ita
(Richard King, *Capuchin Annual*)

Ita was born of noble and apparently Christian parents in about 480 in Co. Waterford. She was first known as Deirdre, before adopting the name Ita as a punning reference to her 'hunger for Divine Love'.

When she reached a suitable age her father sought to arrange her marriage with a noble youth. By dint of her prayers an angel of the Lord appeared to her father, persuading him that she should be permitted to take up the religious life, predicting that 'in another part of the country shall she serve our Lord, and become patron over the race that inhabits it'. Needless to say, her father consented to her taking up the religious life and she set off to seek a place to found her monastery, which was later to be called Killeedy [Ita's Church].

Pious women flocked to her establishment to place themselves under her rule. A local chieftain offered her some land surrounding her monastery, but she accepted only four acres, which she converted into a vegetable garden. She subjected herself to regular, rigorous fasting, frequently spending up to four days without food of any kind. This met with divine disapproval and an agreement was reached whereby she would be miraculously supplied with food from heaven, which she was obliged to consume.

She was endowed with miraculous powers of healing, as when she restored the power of speech to a local wise man, and of prophecy, with a particular ability to detect transgressions, which she used to protect one of her nuns, who was unjustly suspected of theft, and to point out the actual culprit, who immediately forsook the religious life.

Both Brendan of Clonfert and Mochoemog are supposed to have received their early educations in her celebrated school for boys. She is awarded the

18

distinction of being called 'Foster Mother of the Irish Saints' and is recognised as patroness of the Parish of Killeedy.

Ita died in 570 at Killeedy, where her grave is situated at the junction of the nave and chancel of the Romanesque church. The grave is still strewn with flowers by pilgrims in the summer, and her feast day is a local holiday.

Church on Ardoilean, Co. Galway

20 January

FECHIN [FEICHÍN, MO-ECA, MO-FHECA]
of Fore, Co. Westmeath

Fechin was born of noble parents at a place called Bile Feichín in Co. Sligo between 580 and 590. His mother, Lassair, belonged to the royal house of Munster.

Several early 'Lives' exist. He received his education at Achonry in Co. Sligo, under St Nathi. Even at this stage of his life he caused water to flow from dry soil, creating a well, known as 'the well of St Fechin'. On the death of Nathi he left Achonry and went to found monasteries at Fore, Co. Westmeath; Cong, Co. Mayo; Omey Island and Ardoilean [High Island], Co. Galway; Termon-feckin, Co. Louth, and Ballysadare, Co. Sligo.

At Omey he baptised the entire pagan population. Two of his monks died of starvation and the rest of the community was threatened with the same fate until relief was sent by Guaire, King of Connacht.

At Fore, where the number of monks in the community rapidly reached 300, Fechin would not permit women access to the establishment; female servants –

St Fechin (Richard King, *Capuchin Annual*)

19

Cross of Cong
(National Museum of Ireland)

Figures from St Manchan's Shrine

even milk-maids – were totally prohibited. Here too he had an opportunity to repay the kindness of King Guaire. The king's son Ronan, who had become a cleric, had long suffered from a grievous headache for which he had sought a cure from physicians, not only in Ireland, but in Britain as well. Eventually he was advised to visit Fechin at Fore. Through the prayers and blessings of Fechin he was quickly restored to complete health and was able to return to his own monastery.

While visiting the monastery of St Ernan, Fechin silenced a mill which had been a constant source of annoyance to those who lived in the guest-house. At Fore, to mitigate the labours of his monks, he built a mill, powered by a miraculous supply of water, which he is supposed to have hewn with his own hands from the solid rock.

Fechin died at Fore of the yellow plague on 20 January 664 or 665. At the time of Fechin's death St Mullin had a vision that all the demons had been so terrified by the bright light which suffused Ireland that they fled the country for a time.

Of his foundations there survive at Fore the remains of the church; at Cong practically nothing survives, although the superb Cross of Cong is preserved in the National Museum in Dublin. On Omey Island is a small medieval church known as Templefeheen [Fechin's Church]; on Ardoilean are the remains of a small monastic settlement including a church. At Termonfeckin the only remains of the monastery are an early grave-slab and an elaborately carved High Cross. At Ballysadare are ruins of three small buildings, including Teampall Mór Feichín [the Great Church of Fechin], a pre-Romanesque building, later provided with a Romanesque doorway in its south wall.

24 January

MANCHAN
of Lemanaghan, Co. Offaly

Manchan's father was either Daga or, according to some authorities, Innaoi; his mother was Mella. After his victory at Carn Conaill in 642 or 648, Diarmaid, son of Aedh Slaine, granted the site of a church as 'altar-sod' and here Manchan founded his monastery, perhaps with monks from Clonmacnoise.

Of the monastery there survive the ruins of a Romanesque church, north of which are traces of St Manchan's House; while east of the church is St

Manchan's Well, from which an ancient causeway leads to an enclosure with a small pre-Romanesque oratory, which tradition describes as the Cell of St Manchan's Mother, St Mella. A very fine twelfth-century tomb-shaped reliquary, St Manchan's Shrine, is preserved in Boher Catholic Church.

31 January

MOGUE [MOEDOC, M'AODHOG, AODHÁN]
of Ferns, Co. Wexford

Figures from St Mogue's Shrine
(Breac M'Aodhog)

Mogue's father, Sedna, and his mother Eithne, both of noble lineage, had been childless for some time and in their anxiety for an heir they prayed frequently to God. One night while his parents were sleeping, a star descended from the heavens and fell on each of them, as a portent of the future greatness and sanctity of their unborn child. A soothsayer subsequently said to Eithne: 'Woman, thou hast conceived a wonderful son, and he shall be full of God's grace.' In due course the future saint was born on an island in Templeport Lake, Co. Cavan, known as Brackley or St Mogue's Island.

He went to Wales to study under St David and, while there, he performed many miracles – miraculously creating roads through bogs where none had previously existed; restoring a beer-laden wagon and its draught oxen when they tumbled down a cliff; curing the blind, lame and deaf son of a British king.

With his religious education completed, Mogue returned to Ireland and proceeded to found his celebrated monastery at Ferns. While the monastery was being built his disciples complained that there was no water on the site. Mogue instructed them to cut down a certain tree. When they had done so a fountain of crystal-clear water appeared in its place.

On another occasion, when Mogue was about 100 miles from Ferns, he had a vision of one of the monks at Ferns slipping and falling in front of the plough he was using. The saint raised his hand and the oxen immediately stopped in their tracks, thus saving the monk from injury.

Leather satchel of St Mogue's Shrine

Mogue also founded a monastery at Cloncagh, Co. Limerick. He died at Ferns between 625 and 632 and of his monasteries at Ferns and Cloncagh only wells remain – that at Ferns being still known as St Mogue's Well. After his death his remains were enshrined in a bronze casket; this, The Breac M'Aodhog, is preserved in the National Museum, Dublin.

# FEBRUARY

1 BRÍD⋆; BRIDGET⋆; BRIGID⋆; BRIGHID⋆; Cinne⋆; Darluaghach⋆
2 Aithmet; Colman; Finnech⋆
3 Caoilfhionn⋆; COLMAN; Cuanan; Cuanna⋆
4 Ciarán; Cuanna; Lomán
5 Finghin; Liadhnan
6 Colm; Lalloc; Maelfhionnain; Mel; Ronan
7 Aodh; Colman; Fionntán; Maonacan; Meallán; Lomán; Lonán
8 Cera⋆; Colman; Failbhe; FIACHRA; FIACRE; Onchu; Ruidche⋆; Ternoc
9 Athracht⋆; Caireach⋆; Colman; Cronan; Ronan
10 Becga⋆; CRONAN; Derlugha⋆; MO-CHUA; Siollan
11 Coghnat⋆; Dubhan; Etchen; Finnia; GOBNAT⋆
12 Aodhán; Cronan; Cuimin; Damhan; Fachtna; Fionán; Lughaidh; Siadhal
13 Conan; Cuachnat⋆; Donoc; Ermen⋆; Fionán; Modhomhnoc
14 Caomhán; Colman; Mainchín

St Brigid attending to cattle
(Ruth Brandt and Colin Smythe Limited)

1 February

BRIGID [BRIDGET, BRIGHID, BRÍD]
of Kildare, Co. Kildare

A simple St Brigid's Cross

Brigid was born in the mid-fifth century, probably in Co. Kildare. However, in Co. Louth there is a strong local tradition that she was born at Faughart, near Dundalk. Many 'Lives' of St Brigid were written, some of them very early, in Latin or in Irish; other later versions were written in Flemish, German and French as well. Both her father, Dubtach, and her mother, Brocseach, came from noble Leinster families, both, apparently, Christians.

As a child Brigid displayed conspicuous generosity to the poor: on one occasion so great was her largesse that her mother's supply of butter was entirely depleted. Conscious that her mother was about to take stock, the young Brigid prayed to God and the butter was miraculously replenished. A bishop known as Macaille, who lived near her parents' home, is credited with clothing her in the white cloak and veil characteristic of the holy women of the time.

It seems most likely that her first convent was founded at Kildare, on a piece of ground given to her by the King of Leinster, and marked by a large and conspicuous oak tree, which gave its name to the spot – 'The Church of the Oaktree'. This was to become the principal church of the Kingdom of Leinster. It may have been founded on the site of a pagan sanctuary, some of whose traditions were preserved, for example, a perpetual fire, tended by nineteen nuns, was kept burning there until the Dissolution.

The monastery at Kildare was unusual for Ireland in that it was a 'double' monastery – one part for nuns, the other for monks – and ruled over by an abbess and an abbot-bishop.

Brigid earned an enormous reputation for healing the sick, especially lepers. There is a story that on one occasion she was visited by two lepers; the saint blessed some water and instructed the lepers to wash each other with it. One leper was cured first and dressed in clean clothes. He then refused to continue washing his companion, so Brigid did it herself. The one who had been first healed complained that he felt 'sparks of fire settling on his shoulders' – his leprosy had been restored to him as a just reward for his pride and lack of charity. She also imparted the gift of speech to a girl who had been born mute.

Many of her miracles recalled the replenishment of food displayed in her childhood. She also made a practice of securing the release of captives.

There is a story that while she was tending a dying pagan chief she sat praying and plaiting rushes from the floor into a cross. The chief opened his eyes and watched her. He asked what she was doing. She explained to him the meaning of the cross and he was so impressed that he asked to be baptised before he died. From this incident sprang the tradition of plaiting St Brigid's Crosses.

She died about 524 and there is a tradition that, along with Patrick and Columba, she is buried at Downpatrick in Co. Down. She was known as 'The Prophetess of Christ, the Queen of the South, the Mary of the Gael'. Of her monastery at Kildare nothing actually remains, though the fine Round Tower, with its Romanesque porch, marks the site. There is a multitude of churches throughout Ireland, both ancient and modern, dedicated to her. The Shrine of St Brigid's Shoe is preserved in the National Museum in Dublin.

A more complex St Brigid's Cross
(National Museum of Ireland)

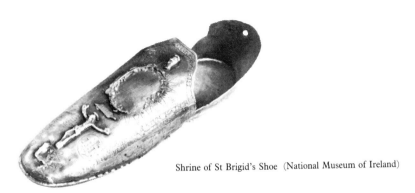

Shrine of St Brigid's Shoe (National Museum of Ireland)

25

3 February

COLMAN [COLMÁN MAC DUAGH]
of Kilmacduagh, Co. Galway

Colman occupied a hermitage at Keelhilla, Co. Galway, where he spent seven years, accompanied only by a single acolyte. At the end of the seven years he had no food left for himself or his attendant. He placed his trust in God and God looked after him.

The Easter banquet being served to his kinsman, King Guaire, in his fortress near Kinvara, was miraculously borne aloft and carried through the air to the hungry Colman. Needless to say, King Guaire followed his floating feast and came upon the saint. So impressed was the King by Colman's piety that he offered him a site for a monastery. And again Colman trusted in God and God found him a site at Kilmacduagh, Co. Galway, and here he founded his monastery. He died in 632.

On Inishmore, in the Aran Islands, another monastery is dedicated to him. Of this there remains a church, Templemacduagh [MacDuagh's Church], a small pre-Romanesque structure. The remains at Kilmacduagh consist of the church, or cathedral, known as Templemore Mac Duagh [MacDuagh's Great Church], a Round Tower and other ecclesiastical buildings. In the cathedral are preserved crude seventeenth-century carvings: The Crucifixion and Saint Colman.

His feast day is also celebrated on 29 October.

8 February

FIACRE [FIACHRA]
of Ullard, Co. Kilkenny

St Fiacre (Ruth Brandt and Colin Smythe Limited)

Fiacre is said to have brought the Last Sacrament to St Comgal of Bangor and he is said to have brought back to Ullard the embalmed arm of St Comgal as a relic.

He went to France, where he died in 670, near Meaux. The site at Saint-Fiacre of his hermit's cell became the nucleus of the great Abbey of Breuil. The Fiacre horse-cab in France was named after him. At Ullard are the remains of a church and the lower part of a High Cross.

St Fiacre's feast day is also celebrated on 30 August.

10 February

CRONAN [MO-CHUA]
of Timahoe, Co. Laois

Cronan studied under St Carthage – Carthach of Lismore – at Rahan in Co. Offaly, and at Lismore in Co. Waterford. He later founded a monastery at Timahoe [Mo-Chua's House] in Co. Laois. He is sometimes confused with another Cronan who was martyred with his monks at Glasmore, Co. Dublin, by the Vikings in 631. However, Cronan of Timahoe appears to have died in 654 or 657.

    The remains of the monastery at Timahoe include fragments of a church and a very fine Round Tower, with a beautiful Romanesque doorway.

Romanesque doorway at Timahoe, Co. Laois

St Gobnat's Church, Ballyvourney, Co. Cork

11 February

GOBNAT
of Ballyvourney, Co. Cork

At some time in the sixth century Gobnat is said to have taken refuge on the Aran Islands, where, indeed, on Inisheer there is a small church called Kilgobnet [Gobnat's Church].

    There is a romantic tale that says that an angel appeared to her there and instructed her to travel until she encountered nine white deer. She founded churches on her way, for example, near Dungarvan, Co. Waterford, until, near Ballyvourney in Co. Cork, she encountered her nine deer and here established her monastery.

St Gobnat (Richard King, *Capuchin Annual*)

27

Wooden statue of St Gobnat

Church at Clonenagh, Co. Laois

She is said to have kept the plague from Ballyvourney by marking the area as consecrated ground across which the plague would not dare pass. There was a field near Ballyvourney called 'the Plague Field' to commemorate this miracle. She is also known as the patroness of bees and on one occasion she is said to have miraculously used a swarm of bees to deter a cattle-raider. At Ballyvourney is still observed the *Tomhas Ghobnata* [Gobnat's measure], where a length of wool is measured against her statue and used for curative purposes.

In the church at Ballyvourney is preserved a much worn wooden thirteenth-century statue of Gobnat, which is displayed to pilgrims on her feast day. The remains of her monastery include the shell of a church, St Gobnat's Grave and St Gobnat's Well. Nearby in Killeen is St Gobnat's Stone, an early cross-pillar, with, on one face, a small crozier-bearing figure.

17 February

FINTAN [FINTAN MOCCU ECHDACH]
of Clonenagh, Co. Laois

Fintan was born in Co. Laois between 525 and 530, according to local tradition. His father was called Gabhren, his mother, Findath, and both were of noble family. Before his birth his mother was visited by an angel who advised her to retire to a secret place, without human contact, until the birth. This she did and, while awaiting the birth, she was miraculously sustained by food from heaven.

The saint studied at Terryglass, Co. Tipperary, at a school established by St Colman. Colman's rule was very strict and he and his monks tilled the ground with spade and hoe. Animal products, such as meat, and even milk and butter, were totally forbidden, to such an extent that a deputation led by St Canice came to visit Colman to beg him to relax his rule. St Comgal of Bangor is said to have been one of his disciples.

Fintan founded his own monastery at Clonenagh on the site of a hermitage of his master. His reputation for recruiting monks, sometimes in a rather unorthodox fashion, was prodigious. For example, he persuaded a man called Fergna, who had a virtuous and beloved wife, twelve sons and seven daughters, 'to abandon this world's pleasures and assume the religious habit'.

Fintan died in 603. Of his monastery only a few mounds now mark the site. His feast day is said to have been also celebrated on 15 November.

18 February

COLMAN
of Lindisfarne

This Colman, with the name borne by nearly one hundred Irish saints, is said to have reigned as one of the last Irish abbots of the Northumbrian monastery of Lindisfarne. But after the Synod of Whitby had decided against the Columban calendar and other Irish monastic practices, he resigned in disgust in 664.

Lindisfarne Priory, Northumbria

The saint went with his followers to Inishbofin in Co. Galway, where he founded a monastery. When disputes arose between his Irish and English followers he founded a separate monastery for the English at Mayo, called Mag nEo na Sachsan [Mayo of the English], from which the county got its name. Colman presided over this monastery, as well as presiding over the one on Inishbofin, until his death between 674 and 676.

All that remains at Mayo is a fragment of ecclesiastical buildings and a trace of the enclosing bank. The site of St Colman's monastery on Inishbofin, close to a fine beach, is marked only by a featureless church and a bullaun stone, which is a large stone with a depression, possibly used as a primitive al fresco font.

20 February

OLCAN [BOLCAN]
of Armoy, Co. Antrim

Olcan's parents are said to have been English. After the death of his father, his mother came to Ireland where she died and was buried in a tomb. A full seven days later a passer-by heard the wails of an infant issuing from the tomb. He rescued the miraculously preserved infant who was later to become the bishop and saint. Olcan is said not only to have been baptised by St Patrick but also to have been consecrated at Dunseverick by him before he founded his monastery at Armoy.

There is a story that a wicked tyrant called Saran overran the territory of Dál

Round Tower at Armoy, Co. Antrim
(R. J. Welch)

Riata [Dalriada], in which Armoy was situated, taking many of its people captive and even vilifying St Patrick. Olcan encountered Saran and the captives and, in order to save the prisoners from certain massacre, he agreed to baptise Saran.

Patrick greatly disapproved of Olcan's so readily baptising an irreligious tyrant without exacting adequate repentance and he predicted that Olcan's church would be polluted with human blood, shorn of its honours and subjected at three different times to destruction. The prophecy was fulfilled when it was sacked in turn by Scandal, King of Dalriada, and Cucuaran, and finally burned by Eochaid.

Of the monastery all that survives is a twelve-metre-high portion of a Round Tower.

21 February

COLMAN [COLMÁN MAC AIDHE]
of Arboe, Co. Tyrone

In the sixth century Colman Mac Aidhe founded the monastery of Arboe, on the shore of Lough Neagh. A very fine, but weathered, High Cross and the remains of Arboe Abbey, as well as a pin-tree in the graveyard, mark the site of his foundation.

This saint's feast day is also celebrated on 18 February.

23 February

FINNIAN [FINNIO MOCCU TELDUIB]
of Clonard, Co. Meath

Finnian was born in Leinster, studied there and later continued his studies in Wales. He came back to Ireland and founded first the monastery of Aghowle in Co. Wicklow. He then went on to found the celebrated monastery of Clonard in Co. Meath, which grew to be one of the pre-eminent monasteries of ancient Ireland, and its school was particularly prestigious. Finnian himself was called 'Tutor of the Saints of Ireland'.

He is credited with numerous books, including a *Life of St Feichín*, none of which has survived.

The sole surviving relic of the monastery at Clonard is a fine fifteenth-century font, now in the Church of Ireland parish church. At Aghowle are the ruins of a twelfth-century church, a cross and an early cross-slab.

The saint's feast day is also celebrated on 12 December.

Church at Killeshin, Co. Laois

27 February

COMGHAN [COMHDAN]

of Killeshin, Co. Laois

Comghan was born in Munster and was one of five brothers – all of whom were renowned for their piety. It is said that when he was dying in the monastery of Killeshin he was told by an angel of the Lord that if the hands of St Ita were laid on his wasting body he would be conducted straight to heaven.

St Ita, with characteristic modesty, protested that he entertained too exalted an opinion of her sanctity, but nonetheless complied with his request. He died some time shortly before 570 – the year of Ita's own death – confident in the belief that her ministrations would secure his eternal happiness.

Of the monastery he founded before the close of the fifth century all that remains are fragments of a Romanesque church with a particularly fine west doorway. The lofty Round Tower was wantonly destroyed in 1703.

Romanesque doorway at Killeshin, Co. Laois

ARCH

1 Baitan; Caisin; Colm; Eanan; Moinenn; Saran; Seanán
2 Conall; Cuan; Feargna; Finnian; Mantan; Slebine
3 Céile Chríost; Cillene; Cillian; Conall; Conna★; Eoghan; Fachtna; Faile★; Mochua; Mosacro
4 Fridolin; Muicin
5 Carthach; CIARÁN; KIERAN
6 AGLENN★; AIGLEND★; Brigid★; Brighid★; Cairbre; Macha★; Nuadhan; Odhrán
7 Cairetan; Meattan★; Mocellach
8 Beodh; Cathal; Ciarán; Conainne★; Conan; Cronan; Mochonna; SENAN; SEANÁN; Siadhal
9 Brighid★; Lughaidh; Mella★; Proinnséas; Séadna
10 Colman; Failbhe; Fearfhuighill; Séadna; Silvester
11 AENGUS; Findchu; Liobran; OENGUS
12 Cillian; Maelcorghais; MURA
13 Camhan; Conchenn★; Cuanghas; Gerald; Mochaemhoch
14 Caomhán; Flannán; Talmach; Ultan
15 Diochuill; Eoghan; Monessa; Neslugh
16 Abban; Aodhán; Felmac; Fionán

17 Beacán; Faoltiarna; Gobban; Lassair⋆; Nessan; PÁDRAIG; PATRICK; Tiarnach

18 Caomhán; Cemán; Conall; Toman

19 LACHTAN; LAICHTAN; LAICHTIN; Mella; Mochua

20 Aodhán; Cathcan; Conan; Mo-Ulloch

21 ÉANNA; EINNE; ENDA; Momhanna⋆; Suirleach

22 Darerca⋆; Failbhe; Liamhan⋆; Trian

23 Beodan; Ciannait⋆; Fearghus; Mainchín; Mocholla

24 CAIMIN; CAMIN; Caorlan; Domhangart; Lughaid; MAC CARTAN; MAC CARTHENN; Mantan; Scire⋆

25 Caimin; Eanan

26 Carthach; Cillian; Cormac; Fintan; Garbhan; Gobhan; Lappan; Mocheallach; Mochta; SINCHEALL; SINCHELL

27 Fionntán; Giolla Mac Leig; Mochonna; Suairleach

28 Cairneach; CASSAN; Conall; Siollan

29 Aodhán; Eithne⋆; Fearghus; Fulartach; Lassair; Sodealbh⋆

30 Colman; Cronan; Fearghus; Tola

31 Colman; Faolán; Fethaidh; Gilda Nachal-Beo; Mella⋆

5 March

KIERAN [CIARÁN]
of Seir Kieran, Co. Offaly

Ruins of the old church at Seir Kieran, Co. Offaly

St Kieran (Richard King, *Capuchin Annual*)

Kieran was, it is said, born in west Cork about the year 375, where, indeed, at Cape Clear he is still revered and there are remains of a church allegedly built by him. He is known as Kieran the Elder to distinguish him from Kieran of Clonmacnoise.

While still young he is said to have gone to the continent to pursue his studies and there to have encountered St Patrick. When he returned he was already ordained and a bishop.

St Kieran settled as a hermit in the Slieve Bloom Mountains at a place then called Saighir, later to become Seir Kieran, his only company being the wild beasts that lived there. It is related that among these was a wild boar who, with his tusks, cut down small branches and other natural materials for the holy man to construct a crude shelter.

Soon, however, he began to attract disciples and Saighir became a thriving monastery. His mother Liadan is said to have brought a group of women to worship under his leadership.

A story about him in his youth describes how on one occasion a hawk swooped down from the sky and snatched a fledgling from a nest. The youthful Kieran was so overcome with pity for the little bird that he prayed for its deliverance. His prayers were answered: the hawk flew down and deposited the little bird, torn and bleeding, at Kieran's feet, where it was miraculously restored to health and strength before his eyes.

His monastery at Saighir prospered and became the burial place of the kings of Ossory, the territory in which it was situated. While at Saighir, Kieran performed many miracles. He was renowned for restoring the dead to life, which he performed several times: once, the dead son of a rich man called Fintan; on another occasion, the seven harpers of Aengus, who had been murdered by brigands; on yet another, a petty chieftain and twenty of his soldiers, restored to life, it would seem, simply because there were insufficient vehicles to remove their bodies for burial. All those so restored became monks under Kieran's rule.

Not all of the saint's miracles were totally beneficent, however. One day Ailill, King of Munster, spoke 'reproachful words' in the presence of the saint. For this he was deprived of the power of speech for a full seven days.

34

Kieran became the patron of the Kingdom of Munster. Of the monastery which Kieran founded, there are extensive ruins, including remains of church-buildings, early grave-stones, a small plain stone cross and the sculptured base of a High Cross with a carving of The Fall and a battle-scene. The west gable of the nearby Church of Ireland parish church contains a weathered figure of St Kieran. Nearby are St Ciarán's [Kieran's] Bush and Stone.

6 March

AGLENN [AIGLEND]
of Killiney, Co. Dublin

Aglenn and her five sisters were daughters of Leinin and therefore sisters of St Colman of Cloyne, Co. Cork. They founded a church here in the sixth century. The church was known as Cill Inghean Leinin [the Church of the Daughters of Leinin], hence Killiney. On the site, there are the remains of an early church with a Greek cross in relief on the west doorway.

Church ruins at Killiney, Co. Dublin

8 March

SENAN [SEANÁN, SENANUS]
of Scattery Island [Inis Cathaig], Co. Clare

Senan was born in the sixth century at Kilrush in Co. Clare, where his family – his father was Ergind and his mother Comgella – was well-to-do. His real-isation that he had a vocation for the religious life came to him one evening when he was guarding his father's cattle by the sea-shore. A mighty wave broke by his feet rather unexpectedly, but then the tide ebbed so that he was able to make his way, dry-shod, across the bay and immediately the waters closed in again. He regarded this as a sign that he should forsake the lay life and so he

Church and Round Tower on Scattery Island, Co. Clare

35

St Senan (Richard King,
Capuchin Annual)

broke his weapon in two pieces and made a cross of it.

He studied at the monastery of Kilnamanagh, near Tallaght in Co. Dublin. He displayed great ingenuity there, by arranging that he could pursue his studies undisturbed, while yet attending to the chores allotted to him. He miraculously automated the mill he was tending so that it functioned successfully without human assistance: the grain obligingly supplied itself and the candle that illuminated his book replenished itself continually.

After his ordination he travelled the country before returning home and establishing his monastery on Scattery Island in the Shannon estuary. When he first visited the island it was in the possession of a great and ferocious monster, breathing fire and spitting venom. Senan was totally undaunted. Protected by the breast-plate of faith, he advanced upon the fearsome beast and made the Sign of the Cross in front of it. The monster was rendered totally unable to move. Senan ordered it to remove itself from the island and never again to harm anyone. The formerly ferocious beast complied.

Senan then observed that the sea around the island could, on occasions, become tempestuous and therefore perilous to those crossing to, and from, it. The angel, who was accompanying Senan, agreed that safe passage would always be arranged for his monks.

Of the monastery he founded the remains include ruins of six churches, one of which is known as St Seanán's Oratory, as well as his grave site. The most spectacular building is the Round Tower, which at nearly forty metres, is the tallest in Ireland.

Pebbles from Scattery are believed to afford protection from destruction by shipwreck. On one recorded occasion a shipwrecked merchant and his brother, who were equipped with the pebbles and believed in their efficacy, were miraculously washed ashore in safety, while their nine companions, not so equipped, were all drowned.

11 March

AENGUS [OENGUS, AENGUS CÉILE DÉ]
of Clonenagh, Co. Laois

Aengus was born some time in the middle of the eighth century, near the monastery of Clonenagh, Co. Laois. His father, Oengoba, was descended from a king of Ireland. From his youth the saint practised extreme asceticism, reciting the entire Psalter every day, part of it while tied by his neck to a stake and immersed to the waist in cold water.

He occupied a hermitage at a place called Dysert [hermitage], near Strad-bally in Co. Laois, before joining the community at Clonenagh, where initially he concealed his true identity. He undertook the most menial and laborious of tasks, and he enjoyed being so employed. Since he was convinced that he was the most abject and contemptible of mortals, and sought to convince others that this was so, he was at no pains to improve his appearance. He allowed his hair to grow long and to be unkempt, and he did not deign to remove from his clothes the dust and the chaff of his labours.

One miracle, which shows a rare affinity with nature, as well as sang-froid of an extreme kind, was performed when he was trimming trees in a neighbour-ing wood. Inadvertently he chopped off his left hand with the axe he was wielding. Immediately the air around was full of birds, all screaming and crying out at the injury to the holy man. To this accompaniment, Aengus, confident in the power and goodness of God, picked up the severed hand and replaced it in its proper position. It instantly adhered, and functioned perfectly as it had done before the accident.

At Clonenagh he began work on his celebrated martyrology, the *Féilire of Aengus*, which he actually finished at Tallaght.

At Dysert are sparse remains of a church. Only a few mounds mark the site of the monastery of Clonenagh. Aengus, however, is remembered most for his work in the *Céile Dé*, or Culdee, reform movement of the Irish Church, and for his literary works. He says in one of his poems:

I am repentant, Lord, for my transgressions, as is right:
Christ, of thy mercy, forgive me for every sin that be attributed to me.

12 March

MURA
of Fahan, Co. Donegal

St Mura's Bell (Wallace Collection)

St Mura is the first recorded abbot of a Columban monastery at Fahan and was patron of the Uí Néill [O'Neills]. He died in 645.

Of the monastic site little survives, but what does remain is of superb

St Mura's Cross, Fahan, Co. Donegal
(Commissioners of Public Works
in Ireland)

quality. The most important, St Mura's Cross, is a flat slab, a little over two metres high. On both faces are ribbon crosses of different designs: that on the west face is flanked by clerics on whose robes can be discerned traces of an inscription in Irish; on the north edge is inscribed a Greek version of the *Gloria Patri*. St Mura's Bell is preserved in the Wallace Collection in London, while his staff, or crozier, is in the National Museum in Dublin.

Distant view of Slemish, Co. Antrim

17 March

PATRICK [PÁDRAIG]
of Ireland

As Patrick himself said:

> Many were reborn in God through me and afterwards confirmed, and clerics were ordained for them everywhere, for a people just coming to the faith, whom the Lord took from the uttermost parts of the earth.

There is no doubt that there were Christian missionaries in Ireland before Patrick's arrival. Kieran the Elder and Ibar seem to have been genuine pre-Patrician missionaries, as was Palladius, who was sent from Rome in 431 as bishop 'to those in Ireland who believe in Christ'. Nonetheless it is certain that it was to Patrick that the Christianisation of Ireland was due.

Patrick was a West Briton and at the age of sixteen he was carried off as a slave by a raiding party and taken to Ireland. Here he spent six years tending herds at a place usually identified with Slemish in Co. Antrim. One night in a dream came the promise: 'Soon you will go to your own country.' He shortly heard the words: 'See, your ship is ready.' At this he left his master and travelled across country until he found a merchant ship preparing to sail.

The ship brought him to a deserted place, possibly in Wales. Eventually he arrived home and was reunited with his family. He did not, however, as might have been expected, adjust well to his good fortune. Again he was subject to disturbing dreams. In one of these he received a letter, 'The Voice of the Irish', beseeching him to return and be with them again.

He went to the continent to receive his education and training, much of it evidently in Gaul, and according to some sources, visited Rome. He is said to have received, while on the continent, the staff known as 'The Staff of Jesus' [*Bachall Íosa*].

He returned to Ireland eventually, traditionally in 432 – a year after Palladius – with several companions. He is thought to have landed first at the mouth of the River Boyne, and then to have travelled north to Saul, where, according to legend, he had his first church, a barn [*sabhall*], given to him by Dichu, the local lord who after first opposing Patrick and even making to attack him with his sword, was miraculously paralysed by the saint. As a result of the awe wrought by this paralysis, Dichu sought baptism and became, with his family, Patrick's first convert in Ireland.

St Patrick

From then on Patrick's mission in Ireland became a triumphal tour around the island, though not totally without hazards. Perhaps his most important early victory was at Tara, the Royal Residence then of King Laoghaire, where he had his celebrated legendary contest with the magician Lucamael.

The first round of the contest was to consist of a trial by water: each was to place his book in water, the winner being the one whose book emerged intact. Patrick was willing but the magician was not. The next round was to be a trial by fire: again each was to place his book in the fire with the winner's emerging unscathed. Again Patrick was willing but the magician was not. The third round resulted in Lucamael being burned to death in part of a specially constructed house, despite the fact that it was made of green wood. In consequence, the conversion and baptism of King Laoghaire and his people took place.

According again to tradition, it was soon after this that Patrick, preaching a sermon on the Holy Trinity on the Hill of Tara, became aware that the concept of the Holy Trinity was difficult for some of the congregation to apprehend and he made use of the shamrock as a visual aid.

The church and churchyard at Saul, Co. Down

He then resumed his tour, converting great numbers of people, many of

The elaborate Shrine of St Patrick's Bell
(National Museum of Ireland)

The simple iron bell for which the shrine
was made (National Museum of Ireland)

whom expressed a wish to be trained for the religious life. Patrick refers to these as 'monks and virgins in Christ'. He established many churches throughout the country, over some sixty of which he placed bishops, in the majority of cases native Irish whom he had consecrated. Many of these churches seem to have been provided with residential accommodation. Only one actual abbot, at Airne in Co. Mayo, and one abbacy, at Drumlease in Co. Leitrim, are specifically named as such.

Patrick performed many miracles in the course of his journey through Ireland. On the mountain in Co. Mayo, later known as Croagh Patrick, he celebrated Easter by fasting for forty days and forty nights. When his fast was coming to an end the air around was suddenly filled with birds, all of an ominous black colour. So thickly gathered were they that the saint could see neither heaven nor earth. The birds were, in fact, demons, and terrific were their screams and fetid was their odour. Patrick continued reciting psalms and hymns and eventually made the Sign of the Cross against them and rang his bell at them – the sound of which, it is said, was heard all over Ireland. He then threw the bell at them and it was cracked in its fall, but the demons dispersed out to the Atlantic. The evil birds were replaced by choirs of angels, in the guise of birds with pure white plumage.

After a lengthy discussion with the angel of the Lord, Patrick succeeded in obtaining all his petitions: that all the Irish would obtain God's clemency; that barbarian invaders would not prevail against the Irish people; that on the Day of Judgment no living person would be in Ireland.

On one occasion a blind man came seeking a cure and, because of his lack of sight, he fell more than once. One of Patrick's company laughed at him. The blind man was cured – the cleric blinded.

Many of the churches founded by St Patrick still exist, often as ruins, others are recalled in the form of place names. Many modern churches, not only in Ireland but throughout the world, are dedicated to him. Of his own writings there has survived his *Confessio*, an explanation of his beliefs. His bell and its shrine, as well as an enshrined tooth, are preserved in the National Museum in Dublin, and his enshrined arm in St Patrick's Church in Belfast.

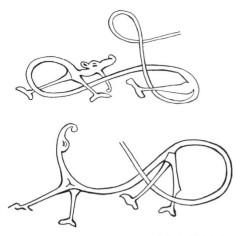

Details of ornament from the Shrine of St Laichtin's Arm

19 March

LACHTAN [LAICHTIN, LAICHTAN, MO-LACHTOG]
of Freshford, Co. Kilkenny

Lachtan was born in west Cork and became a disciple of St Comgal of Bangor. He founded a monastery at Donoughmore in Co. Cork, before founding one at Freshford. He died in 622.

Of his foundation at Donoughmore nothing remains, while a fine late Romanesque doorway from a church on the site of his monastery at Freshford is incorporated in the Church of Ireland parish church there. The handsome – but rather gruesome – *Shrine of St Laichtin's Arm*, which originally belonged to his monastery at Donoughmore, is preserved in the National Museum in Dublin.

Romanesque doorway at Freshford, Co. Kilkenny (Bord Fáilte)

21 March

ENDA [ÉANNA, EINNE]
of Aran, Co. Galway

Enda was born in Meath where his father, Ainmire, was a chieftain. After a military career he succeeded his father as chieftain until his sister Fainche, herself a nun, persuaded him to become a cleric.

A nineteenth-century pilgrimage to a Holy Well

Enda trained in the monastery of Candida Casa at Whithorn in Galloway, Scotland, and he is credited with introducing monasticism, in the strict sense, to Ireland. He established a monastery on Inishmore in the Aran Islands where at Killeany [Cill Einne] are the stump of a Round Tower and parts of a High Cross, and also *Dabhach Einne* [St Enda's Vat], which is actually a well. Nearby is Tighlagheany [St Enda's Household], the holiest place on the island, where 120 saints are said to rest. The visible remains include a small church with part of a High Cross, several inscribed grave-stones and St Enda's Grave. On Inisheer, the smallest of the Aran Islands, overlooking Foul Sound, is Tobereany [St Enda's Well].

24 March

CAMIN [CAIMIN]
of Inishcaltra, Co. Clare

Camin was half-brother of King Guaire Aidhne of Connacht and to him is attributed the foundation of the monastery on Holy Island, or Inis Cealtra, in Lough Derg on the River Shannon.

The remains of the monastery here are the finest in Co. Clare, with earthworks of the earliest monastery, four churches, two High Crosses, a Round Tower and an early cemetery. St Caimin's Church and St Michael's Church both have interesting Romanesque features. A medieval illuminated manuscript, known as *St Caimin's Psalter*, which may have originated in the monastery, is preserved in the Franciscan House of Studies at Killiney in Co. Dublin.

24 March

MAC CARTAN [MAC CÁRTHENN]
of Clogher, Co. Tyrone

According to legend, Mac Cartan was St Patrick's 'Strong Man' and is honoured as the first bishop of Clogher, which appears to have been a pagan sanctuary before he established his see there. Of the monastery all that survives are the remains of two High Crosses and a door-lintel. Apart from one of St Patrick's, St Mac Cartan's is the only Irish liturgical office still surviving.

26 March

SINCHELL [SINCHEALL THE ELDER]
of Killeigh, Co. Offaly

Sinchell founded the monastery at Killeigh which was to become one of the principal churches of Uí Failghe [Offaly]. Indeed the conference of Magh Ailbhe, held in 630 to settle the Easter Controversy, is thought to have taken place in the neighbourhood. Sinchell, who died in 549, is alleged to have reached the unlikely age of 330.

Of the abbey founded by him no trace survives except the Seven Blessed Wells.

28 March

CASSAN
of Donaghmore, Co. Meath

St Patrick himself is supposed to have established the 'great church' [*Domnach Mór*] and to have entrusted it to the care of his disciple Cassan, whose wonder-working relics were venerated here for centuries.

Of the church and subsequent monastery all that survives is a splendid Round Tower, with a Romanesque doorway embellished with a crucifixion and two human masks.

Cross of Clogher (National Museum of Ireland)

43

PRIL

1 Aodhán; Ceallach; Gobban; Tuan

2 BRONACH*; Conall

3 Coman; Cuannan; Faolán

4 Coine*; Colman; Gallus; TIGERNEACH; TIGHERNACH; Ultan

5 Beacán; Tigearnach

6 CATHBAD; Cronan

7 Aodh; Ceallach; FINAN; Ruisin; Seanán

8 Aodhán; Ceannfhealadh; Failbhe; Ronan; Tiarnán

9 Aedhach; Brogan; Colman; Seanán

10 Cuann

11 Aodh; Dadhnan; Maodhog; Seanán

12 Cillin; Conna; Eirnín; Emin

13 Mochaemoc

14 Cillian; Colman; TASSACH

15 Grellan; RUAN; RUADHÁN; Sarnat*

16 Beaccan; Failbhe; Maloc; Miolan; Ultan

17 Domhnall; Donnan; Eochaidh; Garbhán; Lughaidh
18 Eoghan; LAISREN; LASERIAN; Lassair⋆; MO-LAISSE; Moninne
19 Cillian
20 Flann; Maolochtraigh; Sedrachor; Sionnach; Sobhartan
21 Bearach; Maelrubha; Ninidh
22 Ceallachan; Luchan; Rufin; Toma
23 Brian; IBAR; IBHAR; IVAR; Mianach; Suairleach
24 Caoinnete; Diarmaid; Eghneach; Flann
25 Dighde⋆; Mac Caille; Lugna
26 Beacán; Cas; Conán; Cronan; Donal; Indreachtach; Seanán
27 ASSAN; Bain; Fearghus; Leccan; Ultan
28 Caomhán; Caornan; CRONAN; Luightighearna; Suibhne
29 Breaccan; Cuach⋆; Fiachna; DICHU; Domangan; Donnán; Éanán;
    Failbhe; Luicridh; Russen
30 Ciarán; Forannan; Luith⋆; Ronan

2 April

BRONACH
of Kilbroney, Co. Down

Bronach was one of the early saintly women and founded the church at Kilbroney, near Rostrevor, where there are two early stone crosses, one with interlace ornament, the other with a grotesque human mask. Her crozier, or enshrined staff, is preserved in the National Museum in Dublin and her bell in Rostrevor Catholic church.

4 April

TIGHERNACH [TIGERNEACH, TIHERNACH]
of Clones, Co. Monaghan

The shrine known as *Domnach Airgid* from Clones, Co. Monaghan

According to one tradition, Tighernach was the bastard child of the foster-daughter of Eochaidh, a chieftain in Limerick, and a man called Cairbre.

Tighernach was captured by Welsh raiders and taken to Britain. He later escaped and made his way to the monastery of Candida Casa at Whithorn in Galloway, Scotland, where he received his education for the priesthood. He went on a pilgrimage to Rome and is said to have brought from there to his native country relics of the apostles Peter and Paul.

On his return to Ireland he established a monastery at Clones but some sources state that, prior to this, he had been bishop of Clogher in Co. Tyrone.

He was renowned for raising the dead to life, which he performed on several occasions. Once it was Eithne, daughter of the King of Munster, who had killed herself because she had been unwillingly betrothed to a British prince. On another occasion it was no less a person than Duach, Archbishop of Armagh.

St Tighernach died at Clones in 549. Of the monastery there survives a handsome carved High Cross, situated in the Diamond, a Round Tower – now roofless, fragments of a Romanesque church and a tomb.

Round Tower at Clones, Co. Monaghan

6 April

CATHBAD
of Kilmakevit, Co. Antrim

In the *Tripartite Life of St Patrick*, in a section describing the saint's activities in Dalriada, it is recorded that in the territory of the 'Race of Aengus' Patrick erected a church, the direction and possession of which he confided to two of his disciples, Cathbad, a priest, and Deman, a monk. It is likely that this was the church of Kilmakevit [Cill-mo-Chathbad], now in the townland of Markstown.

Because the saint had the same name as Cathbad the Magician, who features in the stories of the *Ulster Cycle*, there was, in the nineteenth century, an amusing confusion among local inhabitants who believed that the founder of the church had been a Druid.

7 April

FINAN [FINAN CAM]
of Kinnitty, Co. Offaly

Finan was a descendant of Connor, King of Ireland. His father was Kennedy, his mother Becnat, and he was born in the middle of the sixth century. When his mother was pregnant with him, wherever she went, no matter how heavily the rain or snow was falling, her garments remained dry.

The saint was a disciple of St Brendan of Clonfert, who advised him to travel to Slieve Bloom where he would meet a herd of wild boars, and there found his monastery. This he did, at a place afterwards to be known as Kinnitty.

On one occasion Finan received hospitality from an old man who had killed the only calf of his only cow to entertain the saint. When Finan learned of this he immediately caused the calf to be replaced.

One very useful feat he performed was for a man who was pressed for time on a long journey. The saint sympathised with his predicament and the man was able to complete a journey that normally would take three days in a mere three hours.

When heavy rain was falling throughout the country, during the harvest, Finan saw to it that not a single drop fell in the fields where his own harvesters were working.

A blacksmith, whose tongs broke as he was working at the forge, asked Finan what he should do. The saint told him to pick up the piece of hot iron in his hand. The smith did so and his hand was completely unharmed. To a boy who was totally paralysed, he also restored the use of his limbs.

Finan is called Cam [crooked] because he apparently had a stoop. Of his monastery all that survives are a few fragments of High Crosses.

Raholp Church, Co. Down (Historic Monuments Branch, Department of Environment for Northern Ireland)

14 April

TASSACH
of Raholp, Co. Down

The church at Raholp was originally founded by St Patrick and entrusted by him to his disciple Tassach, who was also, apparently, a skilled craftsman, making crosses, croziers and bells for Patrick. He is said to have administered the last rites to St Patrick. The church is known as Templemoyle [Teampall Maol].

The extant ruins stand inside an earthen bank and consist mainly of a simple rectangular structure of stone bonded with clay, which is possibly one of the oldest church-structures in Ireland of which anything survives. There are also some genuine early grave-stones.

Ruins of a medieval church at Lorrha, Co. Tipperary

15 April

RUAN [RUADHÁN]
of Lorrha, Co. Tipperary

Ruan was a disciple of St Finnian of Clonard and founded his monastery at Lorrha in the sixth century. It was to become one of the foremost monasteries of Munster. Several 'Lives' of Ruan exist, but there is little reliable information and certainly the famous story of his 'cursing' of Tara is a fiction. However, the story does include a charming tale describing how he protected a petty chieftain who sought sanctuary with him from the High King.

Ruan hid the fugitive in the cellar of his church, and when asked by the High

King about the whereabouts of his quarry, Ruan was able truthfully to answer, 'I don't know, unless he's under your feet!'

Another story tells how, when he was travelling in his chariot one day, some lepers asked him for alms. He presented them with the two horses that were drawing his chariot. Two deer immediately rushed from the forest and took the horses' places until Ruan returned safely to his monastery.

Lepers – twelve of them – figure in another story. When they arrived at the monastery Ruan stuck his staff in the ground and immediately a well gushed forth. The lepers bathed in the water and were cleansed of their leprosy.

The site of Ruan's monastery is now occupied by the Church of Ireland parish church and in the graveyard are the stumps and bases of two High Crosses which were demolished by the Cromwellians. The *Stowe Missal* was removed from Terryglass to Lorrha in the twelfth century and in the fourteenth century its metal shrine was refurbished. It is now preserved in the National Museum in Dublin. St Ruan's Bell is in the British Museum in London.

Shrine of the *Stowe Missal*

18 April

LASERIAN [LAISREN, LAISREN MOCCU IMDE, MO-LAISSE]
of Leighlin, Co Carlow

Laserian is said to have been born in Ulster and to have studied with Fintan of Taghmon. Eventually he came to a monastery at Leighlin, founded in the fifth or sixth century by St Gobban, and he succeeded Gobban as its abbot.

On one occasion he and Gobban went to the gate of the monastery where they met a woman carrying the head of her son who had been killed by brigands. The head was joined to the lifeless body and, through the intercession of Laserian, life was restored to the boy and he was restored to his mother.

Laserian had, apparently, travelled to Rome, where he acquired 'revised' texts of the Gospels and he became versed in the new Roman method of computing the date of Easter. At the Synod of Magh Ailbhe, held in about 630 to consider the dating of Easter, Laserian was the champion of the new method, while his teacher Fintan upheld the traditionalist views.

Laserian died in 639. His monastery became one of the leading foundations in Leinster and, when a formal diocesan structure was adopted by the Irish

St Laserian (Richard King, *Capuchin Annual*)

49

Church in 1110, Leighlin became the see of the diocese to which it gave its name.

The only remains of the monastery are St Laserian's Cross, St Laserian's Well and the pedestal of another cross in the graveyard.

23 April

IBAR [IBHAR, IVAR]
of Beggerin Island, Co. Wexford

Ibar is described as one of the most obdurate of the opponents of St Patrick's Mission, as an independent contemporary missionary. It has been suggested that the main reason for his opposition was that Patrick was a foreigner. Ibar is credited with having established a pre-Patrician church on Beggerin Island, which is also known as Inis Ibair.

There was considerable local devotion to him and pilgrims still visit the site of the early church, of which all that survives are ruins and a few early grave-slabs.

27 April

ASSAN [ASSICUS]
of Elphin, Co. Roscommon

When St Patrick established a church and bishopric at Elphin he entrusted it to his disciple Assan, assisted by the holy matron Cipia, the mother of Assan's nephew and successor Betheus. Assan was credited with being a craftsman.

There is a story that Assan told a lie, but by innocent accident. He was, nonetheless, so shamed by the incident that he fled to a hermitage on Slieve League in Co. Donegal. At the end of seven years his monks discovered his whereabouts and induced him to return to Elphin. On the way back he died at Racoon, Co. Donegal, another Patrician foundation.

28 April

CRONAN
of Roscrea, Co. Tipperary

Cronan was born in Munster and founded his first monastery on the remote promontory of Roscré, on a lake called Lochcré, which was drained away in the late eighteenth century. When he realised that this remote location was inconvenient for visitors, including the poor, he founded a second monastery nearby, which was more accessible. Some visitors, it is said, found the first site so remote that they failed totally to find it.

On one occasion the saint lost a copy of the Gospels in the nearby lake. It remained in the water for a full forty days and nights, but when Cronan, who was greatly concerned at its loss, recovered it, not a single letter of the text had been destroyed.

Of the second monastery the scant remains include an imperfect Round Tower with a Romanesque doorway, a damaged High Cross called the Shrine of St Cronan and the west gable of a Romanesque church. In the pediment of the church is a much-weathered figure of an ecclesiastic assumed to be St Cronan. The illuminated gospel-book, *The Book of Dimma*, now in the library of Trinity College in Dublin, at one time belonged to Cronan's monastery.

St Cronan's Church at Roscrea, Co. Tipperary

29 April

DICHU
of Saul, Co. Down

Dichu is supposed to have been Patrick's first convert in Ireland and it was on his territory that Patrick is said to have landed. At first he opposed the missionary, largely because he thought the saint and his followers were pirates, but he became miraculously paralysed when he attempted to draw his sword against him.

Dichu's subsequent conversion induced him to give Patrick the land for his first church, which in the first instance was a barn, *Sabhall Pádraig* [Patrick's Barn], from which the name Saul is derived.

The scant remains on the site include the foundations of a small church and several early grave-slabs.

MAY

1 Brioch; CEALLACH; Ceallan; KELLACH; Luithrenn*; Mainchín; Natchaoim; Oisín; Ronan; Ultan

2 Colman; Fiachra; Éanán; Neachtan

3 Cairbre; Connlaed; Nem; Sarnat*; Scannall

4 Aodh; Colmoc; Cronan; Mochua; Siollan

5 Faolán; Seanán

6 Colman

7 Aireran; Bearchán; Laisre; Mochiarog

8 Breanainn; Comán; Odhrán

9 Colman; Sanctan

10 Aodh; Cathal; COMGAL; COMHGHALL; Connla

11 Caoimhghin; Findlugh; Fionntán; Laisre*; Lughaire; Mochritoch; Molua; Senach

12 Ailithir; Bearnasca; Conall; Eirnín; Erc; Luan

13 Ceallach; Mochonna; Moeldod; Tiarnach

14 CÁRTHACH; CARTHAGE; Garbhán; Laisre*; Maolcethair; MO-CHUDA

15 Colm; Colman; Comán; Dachonna; Damhnait*; Muireadhach

16 BRANDAN; BRENDAN; BRENANN; Duthracht; Earnán; Fiodhmuine; Odhrán

17 Critan; Finnian; Siollan
18 Aghna★; Bran; Breasal; Colman; Modhomhnoc
19 Ceir; Ciarán; Cuimín; Mochonna; Richeal
20 Colman; Connal; Laidchenn
21 BARRIND; BARRFHIONN; BARUIN; Brighid★; Colman; Cuimín;
    Fionnbharr; Moinne; Rónán
22 Aghna★; Baothin; Conall; Luighseach; Ronan
23 Coman; Criomhthann; Giobhnenn; Moninne★
24 Aibhen; Bearchán; Colman; Derbhile★; Siollan; Stellan; Ultan
25 Donnchadh
26 Beacán; Colman
27 Cillian; Comach★; Cuintoc; Ethian; Moelan
28 Cummain★; Eoghan; Faolán; Furodhran
29 Bruinseach★; Commain; Maeltuile
30 Gobban; Saorgus
31 Coirpre; Eirnín; Eoghan; Maolodhrain

Round Tower at Killala, Co. Mayo

1 May

KELLACH [CEALLACH]
of Killala, Co. Mayo

Doubt has been cast on the very existence of Kellach, except as the starring figure in a tale of treachery and intrigue.

Born about 520, Kellach was the eldest son of Eogan, King of Connacht. He was sent to Clonmacnoise to be educated by St Kieran. So impressed was he with the religious life that he resolved to renounce his heritage and to become a monk. In about 537, however, Eogan was obliged to defend his territory against his rival, Guaire, in a battle fought at Sligo, in which Eogan was mortally wounded. While he lay dying, Eogan persuaded the other Connacht chiefs to elect his eldest son, Kellach, to succeed him – his younger son Cuchoingelt being still a minor.

Envoys were despatched to Clonmacnoise to entreat Kieran to release Kellach from his vows, but Kieran refused. The envoys, however, persuaded Kellach to accede to his father's dying wish, with, or without, Kieran's permission.

Kellach left Clonmacnoise without informing Kieran who was so displeased that he pronounced a malediction on Kellach. Very shortly Kellach began to experience the perils of politics: one of the other Connacht chieftains, Aidhne, resenting his inferior position, revolted, and by a neat piece of treachery routed Kellach's guards and forced Kellach, and twenty-seven of his followers who survived, to take to flight.

Ruing the day he had allowed the envoys to seduce him from the religious life, Kellach retired to a desert place and wept tears of sorrow for abandoning

Christ's service. After a year of this self-imposed penance he went to Clonmacnoise, where Kieran eventually received him and a reconciliation was achieved. Kieran, however, pointed out that he could not withdraw the malediction.

In about 544 Kellach was appointed Bishop of Killala. Even here, in his religious office, he was not safe from political intrigue. He was suspected of supporting the claims of his brother Cuchoingelt and, although he attempted to take refuge in a hermitage with four followers, they were hacked to pieces in a thicket.

Of the monastery where St Kellach served as bishop there only remains a very handsome Round Tower.

10 May

COMGAL [COMHGHALL]
of Bangor, Co. Down

St Comgal (Richard King, *Capuchin Annual*)

Comgal was born in Dál nAraide [Dalaradia], probably near Magheramorne in Co. Antrim, between 515 and 520. St Patrick, some sixty years previously, had foretold of his birth.

The day before Comgal's birth Mac Nisse of Connor heard a chariot passing and observed to his followers, 'This chariot carries a King.' When he and his followers looked out, the only chariot they could see was occupied by a man called Sedna and his pregnant wife Briga, both well known to them. Mac Nisse insisted that his first observation had been right: 'That woman bears a King; he shall be adorned with all virtues and the world shall be illuminated with the lustre of his miracles.'

In due course Briga gave birth to Comgal. He went to study under St Fintan of Clonenagh in Co. Laois. Here he restored sight to a blind man by applying saliva to his eyes in the name of Christ. He eventually returned to his own part of Ireland and established his monastery at Bangor on the shores of Belfast Lough, or Lough Lee as it was then called, in or about 555. It is said that at one time there were 4,000 monks with the grace of God under the yoke of Comgal at Bangor. It was known as 'The Vale of the Angels' and later described by St Bernard of Clairvaux as being 'truly sacred, the nursery of saints'.

Although he himself was reputed to eat a full meal only on Sunday, several of

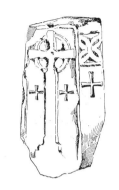

Cross-slab from Bangor Abbey, Co. Down

Bell of Bangor (Ulster Museum)

Comgal's miracles are concerned with food. One involved a group of thieves who were in the habit of stealing fruit and vegetables from the monastery garden. One night Comgal prayed to God to deprive them of sight until they were ready to confess their crime. Accordingly the thieves came to the garden and were immediately blinded. They stumbled around unable to find an exit and finally started to cry for help. They were truly penitent and made reparation. They were forgiven and shortly afterwards placed themselves under Comgal's rule.

On another occasion the monastery ran short of grain, while a nearby farmer called Croidhe had an abundance. Unfortunately Croidhe had an exceedingly mean nature. When the monks went to visit him, seeking to buy some grain, he nastily refused to sell them any, saying sarcastically that he'd rather it was eaten by Luch, his mother, than let the monks have it. The word *luch* means 'mouse' and Comgal said cunningly: 'So be it, by *luch* it shall be eaten.'

That night two heaps of Croidhe's corn, amounting to thirty wagon loads, were duly eaten by mice.

There is also the incident of Comgal's vision that Columba and some of his monks were about to visit. Since the monastery was short of food Comgal requested divine assistance. Immediately a large shoal of fish swam close in to shore, were caught and taken to the monastery to feed the guests.

In his later days Comgal became increasingly infirm, and when it became obvious that his end was rapidly approaching, his monks asked him to let them administer the last rites. Comgal declined, saying that he would wait until St Fiacre of Ullard, in distant Kilkenny, arrived. An angel of the Lord visited Fiacre and despatched him to Bangor where he duly did administer the last rites to Comgal. He also brought Comgal's arm back to Ullard as a relic to be enshrined. Comgal died in 601 or 602.

Among the many famous Irish missionaries who trained in Bangor and went on to labour on the mainland of Europe were Columbanus of Luxeuil in France and Gall of St Gall in Switzerland.

While nothing remains *in situ* of this famous foundation, an extremely important relic, in the form of a small service-book known as *The Antiphonary of Bangor*, is preserved in the Ambrosian Library in Milan, in Italy. The decorated Bell of Bangor is preserved in the Heritage Centre in the town.

Romanesque doorway at Rahan, Co. Offaly

14 May

CARTHAGE [CÁRTHACH, MO-CHUDA]
of Lismore, Co. Waterford

The birth of Carthage was announced, in advance, to both St Comgal of Bangor and St Brendan of Clonfert. He was born in Kerry of a rich family; his father was Fingen and his mother Maeve. He was baptised by a holy man called Aedan; there was no water at the spot, but instantly a fountain burst forth and its waters were used for the ceremony.

One day while he was tending herds a bishop, with his followers, went past singing psalms. Carthage was entranced and followed them and remained outside the monastery all night, listening. Soon he joined the community of the bishop, who was Carthage the Elder, and with him was advanced to ordination. On the advice of his master, Carthage retired to a remote hermitage in south Kerry, but left it because of dissension with two local bishops, and set off on a pilgrimage to the northern part of Ireland.

While there he spent a year with Comgal of Bangor before returning to Kerry and, after a while, he found his way to Rahan, Co. Offaly, where he spent many years. During this period he performed a number of miracles. A local wizard challenged the saint to make leaves appear on an apple tree: this was speedily done; then the wizard demanded blossom: this too was achieved; then the wizard demanded fruit: this also was produced, but the wizard complained that it was very bitter. The saint sweetened the apples and then blinded the wizard for a year for his lack of faith.

On another occasion a poor neighbour came to the monastery to see if he could borrow a plough and two oxen. The monks, however, did not use a plough – they tilled with hoes and spades. Carthage sent one of his monks into

St Carthage

57

the forest to fetch two deer. When the poor man's ploughing was finished the deer returned to the forest.

The spirit of obedience generated by Carthage's rule is amply demonstrated by an occasion when a monk, who was supervising some work near a river, called for another named Colman to enter the water to carry out some necessary task. Immediately twelve monks, who happened to share the same name, rushed, fully clothed, into the water.

Towards the end of his life the saint was expelled from Rahan at Easter of 636, at the instigation of the community of Durrow. He and his monks, as well as a group of lepers, to whom Carthage had given succour, set off seeking a site for a new monastery. He was offered a site by the King of Cashel, but Carthage refused because this was not the spot that God had indicated. Eventually they reached the River Blackwater and the monastery of Lismore was established. He died at Lismore in 636 and is buried there.

Of the monastery at Rahan there survive some earthworks and three small churches. The largest of these serves as the Church of Ireland parish church. It retains a fine and unusual Romanesque arch between the nave and chancel, as well as a unique circular Romanesque east window. The other two churches are roofless ruins; while one is a featureless primitive structure, the other is a plain pre-Romanesque building into which a beautiful Romanesque west doorway has been inserted.

Of the monastery at Lismore, which in its heyday boasted no fewer than twenty churches, only a few poor fragments survive. In the Church of Ireland Cathedral is an elaborate sixteenth-century tomb, which includes a figure of St Carthage.

One of the surviving ruined churches at
Rahan, Co. Offaly

16 May

BRENDAN [BRANDAN, BRENANN 'THE NAVIGATOR']
of Clonfert, Co. Galway

Brendan was born in Kerry, some say at a place called Fenit, near Tralee, the son of Finlogue, towards the end of the fifth century. His birth had been predicted by St Patrick and on the night that he was born the whole area around the house was brilliantly illuminated while angels hovered over it. A local Bishop called Erc baptised him. He remained with his parents for only one year after his baptism. He was then put to fosterage with St Ita at her monastery in Co. Limerick for five years.

The saint then went to Bishop Erc to continue his education, accompanying him on visitations when he reached the age of ten. After some time he expressed a desire to travel through Ireland and meet some of the other holy men. Erc gave him his blessing, but implored Brendan to return to him so that he could perform his ordination.

Brendan studied under Finian of Clonard for a time, and then spent some more with Jarlath of Tuam. He duly returned to Erc for his ordination and even at this early stage attracted disciples.

Early in the sixth century an Irish monk called Barrind had voyaged out into the Atlantic Ocean with some companions and found a distant and beautiful land before returning to Ireland. Barrind came to visit Brendan one evening and told him of his journey to the land he described as 'The Land of Promise of the Saints'.

Barrind's description fired Brendan with ambition to visit this far-off land himself. He and his monks fasted for forty days and nights, after which he set

St Brendan, his companions and the whale

St Brendan and the creatures of the sea
(Robert Gibbings)

off for the Aran Islands where he met Enda, with whom he remained for three days, seeking information.

Returning to Kerry, Brendan and his chosen companions prepared their vessel and set off on their voyage. After forty days their food was exhausted. They spied an island, but could find no accessible anchorage.

Eventually, after circling the island for three days, they did find a landing place and disembarked. They found accommodation and food prepared for them. They then voyaged on and found another island. On this too they found abundant nourishment, in the form of plenteous sheep. The next island they encountered caused some consternation, because as soon as they lit a fire on it, it moved. Brendan explained to his monks that they had, in fact, landed on a whale.

After they had voyaged for seven years, encountering many wonders and finding many lands and islands, they at last became homesick and returned to Ireland, having visited what we now call Iceland, Greenland and, probably, America as well.

On his return from his legendary voyage Brendan founded his monastery at Ardfert, where disciples flocked to join him. He seemed to suffer from a sort of wanderlust, for he shortly afterwards set off on a pilgrimage that took him not only to Wales but, apparently, to Brittany as well.

On his journey home to Ireland he observed two monsters of the deep alternately fighting and swimming, one of them clearly getting the worst of it. Brendan heard it cry out in a human voice: 'I claim the protection of St

Patrick.' To which the other replied: 'St Patrick's protection will avail you not.' And the first cried out again: 'I claim the protection of St Brendan.' To which the reply was: 'St Brendan's protection will avail you not.' Finally, the weaker cried out: 'I claim the protection of the Holy Virgin Brigid.' At this the stronger gave up the contest and swam off.

Brendan was most impressed by this demonstration of the potency of Brigid's sanctity and, when he went to visit her, he asked how it came about. She explained that it was simply because she devoted her whole life and all her attention to God.

It was not until he was seventy-seven that Brendan eventually founded his celebrated monastery of Clonfert. It was at Clonfert that he had a conversation with Michael the Archangel, in the guise of a bird. He died at an advanced age in 577.

Brendan's fantastic voyage is the subject of a medieval tale, *Navigatio Sancti Brendani* [The Voyage of St Brendan], which was translated into practically every European language.

The site of his monastery at Ardfert is marked by St Brendan's Cathedral, into which is incorporated a fragment of a Romanesque church. At Clonfert the doorway of St Brendan's Cathedral is one of the glories of Irish Romanesque architecture.

Romanesque doorway at Clonfert, Co. Galway (Commissioners of Public Works in Ireland)

21 May

BARRIND [BARUIN, BARRFHIONN]
of Kilbarron, Co. Donegal

Barrind was born in the north of Ireland, early in the fifth century. His father was called Muredoc and his mother Didhuat. He was a relative and colleague of St Columba.

He founded a church at Drumcullen in Co. Offaly and then one at Kilbarron in Co. Donegal. This saint has been identified with the Barrind who voyaged to the 'Land of Promise of the Saints' and, by his description of his adventures, he inspired Brendan of Clonfert to make his celebrated voyage.

At Drumcullen there are the remains of the abbey and the head of a High Cross, while at Kilbarron the site is marked by a small medieval church.

Church ruins at Kilbarron, Co. Donegal

UNE

1 Colman; Cronan; Cuimín; Egol; Liban; Ronan; Stellan
2 Aodhán; Colman; Conall; Luran; Ninnidh; Seanán
3 Aiffen; Brandubh; CAOIMHGHIN; CAOIMHÍN; KEVIN; Mochua; Moninne⋆; Sillan
4 Breague; Cassan; Colm; Colman; Eirnín; Faithleann; Finchan; Lua
5 Bearchán; Findlugh; Lean; Loban; Niadh
6 Caemhan; Cocca; Colman; Faolán; IARLAITH; JARLATH; Lonán
7 Caomhán; COLMAN; MO-CHOLMOG; Mochonna
8 Bron; Luaithren⋆; Meadhran
9 Baethin; COLM; COLMCILLE; COLUMBA
10 Ainmire; Bearach
11 Eoghan; Riaghail; Toccomhracht
12 Caomhán; Cronan; Cunera⋆; Giolla Chríost; Lochen; Torannan
13 Coireall; DAMHNAT⋆; DAMNAT⋆; DAVNET⋆
14 Ciarán
15 Colman

St Kevin's Church at Glendalough, Co. Wicklow

3 June

KEVIN [CAOIMHGHIN, CAOIMHÍN]
of Glendalough, Co. Wicklow

Kevin was born in east Leinster of parents of noble birth – his father was called Coinlogha and his mother Coenhella. There is a story that to lead a more pious life they renounced their inheritance and were sustained by the labour of his father's hands. During Kevin's infancy a white cow appeared miraculously at his parents' house every morning and evening, giving two large vessels of milk every day without fail.

He received his early training at the monastery of Kilnamanagh, near Tallaght in Co. Dublin, under Saints Eogan, Lochan and Enda. There is a story that while studying there he was pursued by a most beautiful maiden who sought to entice him from his celibate life. On one occasion he concealed himself in a bed of nettles; she followed him relentlessly until he repelled her by striking her with a bundle of nettles. This treatment appears to have had the effect desired: she immediately repented and lived the rest of her life in purity and sanctity.

Kevin retired from the world to live as a hermit in a most isolated spot in a wilderness among the Wicklow mountains. Such was his reputation that against his wishes disciples flocked to him in ever-increasing numbers, eventually making it necessary for the community to move to a more spacious site on the eastern side of the upper lake at Glendalough. It was Kevin's practice to remove himself from the community during Lent, and there is a particularly charming story about an incident during one of these periods of solitude.

One day he was kneeling in his tiny cell, with his hand stretched out through the little opening that served as a window. A blackbird flew onto it and, settling herself, she eventually laid her egg in his open hand. So patient, kind and gentle was he that he remained kneeling until the egg was hatched and the fledgling grown.

His monastery grew and its fame grew with it, soon becoming a place of pilgrimage – a pilgrimage to Glendalough being thought the equivalent of one to Rome. He died about the year 620.

The remains of the monastic settlement are extensive, scattered over a mile and a half of the valley of Glendalough. The site of Kevin's original hermitage [Dísert Chaemhghin] is occupied by Templenaskellig, several early

St Kevin (Robert Gibbings)

graveslabs, a platform which may be the site of domestic cells, a small cave known as St Kevin's Bed, and St Kevin's Church and Reefert Church. Between these and the larger site are a series of rather plain crosses. The later monastery includes the Cathedral – the largest church in the complex – St Kevin's Church, St Mary's Church and St Kieran's Church, as well as a Round Tower.

6 June

JARLATH [IARLAITH]
of Tuam, Co. Galway

Jarlath was taught at Kilbennan, Co. Galway, by Bennan [Benignus], before establishing his monastery at Tuam in the fifth to sixth century. The ecclesiastical importance of his foundation grew and by the Reformation it boasted two monasteries and three churches: the Cathedral, St Iarlaith's Church, and Teampall na Scríne, where Jarlath's relics were enshrined.

St Jarlath (Richard King, *Capuchin Annual*)

Of the early buildings little remains, although a fine arch and window in the Church of Ireland Cathedral are outstanding examples of Irish Romanesque architecture. There are fragments of two High Crosses, one in the Cathedral, the other in the Market Place.

7 June

COLMAN [MO-CHOLMOG]
of Dromore, Co. Down

This Colman's birth is said to have been predicted by St Patrick and he is said to have studied at Nendrum, Co. Down, as well as being a close friend of St Mac Nisse of Connor, before founding his monastery at Dromore in the sixth century. One of the miracles credited to him is restoring life to the future St David of Wales, who, according to this story, was still-born.

Finian of Movilla is said to have studied at Dromore, as did many missionaries who went to Scotland and Wales, leaving monasteries named after their teacher, like Innis mo Cholmaig in Scotland and Llangolman in Wales, for example.

One of the High Crosses at Tuam, Co. Galway

The only surviving relics of his foundation at Dromore are the High Cross in the Market Place and an early grave-slab, known as St Colman's Pillow, in the Church of Ireland Cathedral.

9 June

COLUMBA [COLM, COLMCILLE]
of Iona, Scotland

Distant view of the monastery on Iona, Scotland

Columba was born at Gartan in Co. Donegal, in or about 520, the son of Felim and his wife Eithne, both of whom were of very noble descent. His coming was predicted by many earlier saints, including St Patrick. An angel attended his mother during his birth.

He studied under the celebrated Finian of Movilla, in Co. Down, before founding the monastery at Doire Calgach [Calgach's Oakwood], later to be known as Doire Cholm Cille, which was to become the site of the modern City of Derry or Londonderry, in 546.

The saint then went on to found monasteries all over Ireland, the most notable of which were at Durrow, Co. Offaly; Kells, Co. Meath; Moone, Co. Kildare, and Glencolmcille, Co. Donegal, before going to Iona [Í Cholm Cille] and founding the monastery there, for which he is most famous, and setting out to Christianise – or re-Christianise – the people of Scotland.

In his youth, Columba's guardian angel informed him that he was permitted to choose his virtues: Columba chose virginity and wisdom. So rightly had he chosen that he was also awarded the gift of prophecy.

On one occasion his companions observed that Columba seemed very sad. They asked why and he replied:

> My Irish people are to me a cause of sorrow, since in time to come they will wage war on one another, will injure, hate and wickedly slay, will shed innocent blood.

He was an accomplished scribe. It was his copy of a manuscript by Finian that lead to the famous judgement 'To every cow its calf, to every book its copy', meaning that the copyright belonged to Finian, who retained the copy as well as the original.

The exile that took Columba to Iona was self-imposed, as a mitigation of a sentence of excommunication arising from a dispute with the High King. A verse from a poem he is supposed to have written on leaving Ireland goes:

There is a grey eye that ever turns
To Erin, across the grey waters.
But never shall it see the sons
Of Erin in this life, nor her daughters.

His successor as Abbot of Iona, Adomnan, who was also Columba's biographer, describes how, just before he died, he travelled in a cart to make a last visit to the fields in which his monks were working. He blessed the grain and stopped at a cross and the old white horse that was there laid its head on his shoulder and wept. He died at Iona in 597. His remains are supposed to have been transferred to Downpatrick in Co. Down, to join those of St Patrick and St Brigid, as St Patrick had foretold.

Of his monastery at Derry, nothing survives; the remains were used by Sir Henry Docwra in 1600 to provide material for his fortifications, except for the Round Tower, which survived until at least 1625. Of his foundation at Durrow a fine High Cross, a few early grave-slabs and St Colmcille's Well mark the site. The celebrated *Book of Durrow*, one of Ireland's most important illuminated manuscripts, now in the Library of Trinity College in Dublin, belonged to this abbey.

Scenes from Columba's life (Margaret Gregory and Colin Smythe Limited)

To remind us of his important foundation at Kells there are five High Crosses, a roofless Round Tower, and a stone-roofed church known as Teach Choluim Chille [Columba's House]. There are also, of course, the best known of the illuminated Gospel books, the magnificent *Book of Kells*, now in the Library of Trinity College in Dublin, and The Kells Crozier, now preserved in the British Museum in London. At Moone is an exceptionally fine High Cross and fragments of another. At Glencolmcille are some early stone crosses, some of which are 'stations' in a three-mile-long *turas* [pilgrimage], held every year on St Columba's Day.

13 June

DAVNET [DAMHNAT, DAMNAT]
of Tedavnet, Co. Monaghan

Davnet founded a monastery for women in Co. Monaghan in the sixth century. Because her name is sometimes Latinised as Dympna she has been confused with Dympna of Gheel in Flanders, patroness of the insane.

Her crozier, known as *Bachall Damhnait*, now preserved in the National Museum in Dublin, was formerly kept in the parish and was used for testing

The Twelve Apostles from the High Cross at Moone, Co. Kildare (Commissioners of Public Works in Ireland)

Churchyard at Tedavnet, Co. Monaghan

the truth of oaths. The punishments for swearing a false oath on the relic were held to be dire – the most usual being the turning awry of the mouth of the bearer of false witness, which would, of course, have the effect of marking him, or her, for life as a liar. Many suspects confessed to crimes they had previously denied when threatened with swearing on the crozier.

17 June

MULLIN [MULLING, MO-LING, DAIRCHELL]
of Saint Mullin's, Co. Carlow

Mullin's father, Faolan, is said to have been a farmer who accumulated considerable wealth. An angel of the Lord is supposed not merely to have been present at the saint's birth, but also later to have returned and baptised him. Mullin seems to have changed his name from Dairchell when, at an early stage, he embraced the monastic life and established his monastery on the River Barrow at the place that later was to be known as Saint Mullin's.

He kept himself apart from his community, living in a small secluded cell and devoting himself to prayer. He did visit the community at intervals, however, and is supposed not only to have established a mill for the service of the monastery, but also to have introduced rye to Ireland.

One day he was observed by one of his monks actually walking, dry-shod, on the waters. He is, moreover, credited with single-handedly digging a channel seven miles long to bring water to his monastery.

Church ruins at Saint Mullin's, Co. Carlow

One night he sent his fishermen to cast their nets for fish. They caught a very large salmon, and when they split it open they found inside a very large gold ring. Mullin divided the gold into three parts, one for the poor, one to make reliquaries and one for the payment of labour.

He is celebrated too for his kindness to animals. On one occasion a group of thirty weary and hungry hounds came to the monastery. Mullin ordered them to be impounded while food was being prepared for them. He instructed his monks to prepare thirty buttered loaves to be distributed among them. While the food was being prepared fifteen of the hounds escaped. Mullin told his monks to give all thirty loaves to the remaining hounds. This they did and each hound took only one loaf and ate it, leaving the others. Shortly afterwards the other hounds returned and each took its share. All the hounds then expressed their gratitude to the saint by wagging their tails.

68

On another occasion he not only rescued a wren that had been eaten by a cat, but also rescued a fly that had been eaten by the wren. He died in 696 and was buried in his monastery.

The Church of Ireland parish church impinges on the site of the monastery, where Mullin's House [Teach Mo-Ling] consists of a small nave-and-chancel church and a two-apartment building, attached to the stump of a Round Tower, known as Mullin's Abbey, as well as a damaged High Cross. The site is also marked by St Mullin's Well and the remains of the saint's mill. A seventh-century enshrined Gospel-book, known as the *Book of Mulling*, is preserved in the Library of Trinity College in Dublin.

23 June

MAHEE [MOCHAOI]
of Nendrum, Co. Down

While serving as a swineherd, Mahee is supposed to have been encountered by St Patrick early in the days of the saint's mission. Perhaps because he recalled his own youthful employment, Patrick converted, baptised and recruited Mahee to his team.

Shortly after, as St Patrick and his followers were conducting a discourse on religious subjects, a pastoral staff descended from heaven and came to rest with its point on Mahee's breast and its crook on St Patrick's bosom. This was regarded as an undeniable sign from heaven.

Ruins of the Round Tower at Nendrum, Co. Down

Forthwith Mahee was consecrated before proceeding to establish his monastery of Nendrum on the island in Strangford Lough named after him. One rather improbable story about him relates that he was lulled to sleep by a bird for three hundred years. He died in 496.

The remains of his monastery were cleared of undergrowth in 1922–4, and rather clumsily excavated. These ruins probably constitute the best surviving example of an early monastic site on the Irish mainland. The remains include three surrounding walls which divide the site into three activity-areas.

In the innermost area are the reconstructed remains of the church, the graveyard and a stump of the Round Tower. In the middle one are traces of domestic cells or huts and of the workshop or scriptorium. The outermost was devoted to the crops and livestock maintained by the monks. Finds from the excavations, now in the Ulster Museum in Belfast, include the iron bell of the monastery, some domestic equipment, and various items from the workshop.

Reconstruction of the monastery at Nendrum, Co. Down (Historic Monuments Branch, Department of Environment for Northern Ireland)

 ULY

1 Ailioll; Cathabh; Conán; Cuimín; Eirnín; Lughaid; Ultan
2 Ternoc
3 Breacnat; Cillian; Dartine★; Maolmhuire; Ultan
4 Fionbarr; Olcan
5 Éadaoin★; Fearghus; Ultan
6 BLINNE★; DARERCA★; Eithne★; Flann; MONINNA★; MONINNE★; SARBHILE★
7 Caoimhghell★; Croine★; Fiadhar; MAELRUAIN; MAOLRUAIN; MULROON; Tiarnach
8 Aedh; Broccan; Cillian; Colman; Diarmaid; Tadg
9 Broccaidh; Condmach; Garbhán; Onchu
10 Aodh; Cuan; Seanán; Ultan
11 Colman; Drostan; Failbhe; Lonán; Oliver
12 Colman; Nasan; Ultan
13 Carreall; Eirnín; Erc; Fionntán; Greallan; Mo-Siollach
14 Colman; Fachtna; Onchu
15 Comman; Ronan

16 Brecan; Maolodhran; Scoth★; Sinach; Tenan; Torbach

17 Flann

18 Ceallach; Cronan; Failbhe; Fionntán; Mianach★

19 Aodhán; Ciarán; Colman; Fearghus; Oisín

20 Carman; Cuirbhin; Failbhe; Faolchu

21 Curcach★; Luan; Siollan; Tenna

22 Buadan; Buite; Colman; Oisín

23 Banbhnat★; Caencomhrac; Foillan; Runach

24 Comhghall; Cronan; DÉAGLÁN; DECLAN; Fachtna

25 Caolán; Colman; Fiachra; Fionnbarr; NEASSAN; NESSAN

26 Toman

27 Beoghan; Breanainn; Dioraid; Guaire; Luit★

28 Comhghall; Forodhran; Liucan

29 Caolán; Comán; Cuimín

30 Cobhthach; Cobuir; Maoltuile; Saran; Sensa

31 Colman; Iarnoc; NAAL; NADAL; NADAN; NATALIS; NOTAN

Church at Killevy, Co. Armagh (Historic Monuments Branch, Department of Environment for Northern Ireland)

6 July

DARERCA [MONINNE, MONINNA, BLINNE, SARBHILE]
of Killevy, Co. Armagh

Darerca was born in the early part of the fifth century, probably in the northern part of Co. Louth. Her father was called Mochta and her mother Coman. She is said actually to have been baptised by St Patrick, who entrusted her to a priest living nearby for instruction. Her original name is said to have been Darerca, or Sarbhile, but Blinne is a name locally applied to her. There is a story which explains how she came to be known as Moninne. Through her intervention a mute poet was given the power of speech and his first utterance was 'Ninne, Ninne', hence Moninne.

Her first community, consisting of a widow with a child and eight virgins, was established near her home at Faughart, Co. Louth, the supposed birthplace of St Brigid. Here they remained for some time, until Darerca found the social intercourse with her friends and relations an excessive distraction from her religious life. She and her nuns, therefore, decided to journey down to the extreme south of Ireland, to Beggerin Island in Co. Wexford, where they lived under the rule of St Ibhar, a precursor and rival of St Patrick.

After her sojourn with St Ibhar she went to stay with St Brigid for a while, because of the fame of Brigid's piety and goodness. Here she served as portress to the hospital and was endowed with the gift of healing the infirm and the possessed. Her reputation as a benefactress to the poor and needy inevitably caused great numbers of them to flock to her door. They always left laden with her bounty, to such an extent that her nuns complained they were left with little or nothing. She replied that if they placed their faith in the Lord, he would compensate for their generosity.

As if to prove her point, that very night twelve beautiful dresses, a gift from heaven, were lying on her bed. These, on the advice of Brigid, she distributed among her nuns. A pauper who was present scoffed at the notion that the dresses were, in fact, a gift from heaven and for his lack of faith he was suddenly struck dead.

After her stay with Brigid, Darerca and her nuns travelled back to the North, where she established her nunnery on the north foot of Slieve Gullion, at a place to be known as Killevy. Here again, as before, her generosity to strangers often left her little community short of supplies. They kept their few cattle on the hillside and one day a calf was carried away by a wolf, only to be returned shortly, miraculously unscathed.

The site of her establishment at Killevy is marked by two conjoint, but not interconnecting, churches. There was once also a Round Tower.

7 July

MAELRUAIN [MAOLRUAIN, MULROON]
of Tallaght, Co. Dublin

Maelruain was born around the beginning of the eighth century and, although we know his father was called Colman and his mother Broicseach, we do not know where he was born, or even where he received his religious education, though it has been stated it was with Fer-da-Crich, Abbot of Dairinis in Co. Cork.

The site of his monastery at Tallaght was given to him by the King of Leinster in 769. Alarmed at the laxity of monastic discipline, then becoming apparent in the Irish Church, Maelruain imposed on his monks a very strict rule. For example, at Tallaght meat and ale were totally forbidden and a fast imposed every month. With strict rules of devotion, obedience and poverty he combined a great interest in scholarship and literature, and he became closely identified with the eighth-century ascetic and intellectual reform movement in the Irish Church, known as the *Céile Dé*, or Culdee, movement.

Associated with Tallaght in this movement were the monasteries of Terryglass, Finglas and Clonenagh. An aphorism credited to Maelruain is:

Do not eat until you are hungry.
Do not sleep until you are ready for it.
Speak to nobody without cause.

Maelruain died in 792.

The monastery of Tallaght is possibly best remembered by the two celebrated works of scholarship compiled there, at least in part: the *Martyrology of Tallaght* and the *Martyrology of Aengus*.

Of the monastery itself all that remains today, both in the grounds of the Church of Ireland parish church, are St Mulroon's Stone, a small plain granite cross, and St Mulroon's Losset, a large crude granite basin.

St Declan's Church on the cliff, Ardmore, Co. Waterford

24 July

DECLAN [DÉAGLÁN]
of Ardmore, Co. Waterford

St Declan (Richard King, *Capuchin Annual*)

Declan was a pre-Patrician missionary, born, it is said, in Co. Waterford. Accounts of his life contain many incompatible facts. It is said that his father was called Erc, his mother Dethidin, and that his birth was attended by spectacular and miraculous phenomena.

Because of his saintly future his mother suffered none of the usual pains of childbirth and a great globe of light was suspended over the roof-top. A Christian priest in the area, Colman, baptised Declan and recommended that when he attained the age of seven 'he should be sent for instruction to a lettered Christian, if such a one could be found'.

Shortly after Declan's birth seven men, who lived nearby and who had witnessed the great globe of light, visited the saint's house and they exclaimed prophetically that he would be their future bishop. They then offered themselves and their habitations to him.

74

Round Tower and St Declan's Church, Ardmore, Co. Waterford (Commissioners of Public Works in Ireland)

When Declan reached the age of seven a religious and wise man called Dymma – an Irishman who had been abroad and had embraced Christianity – arrived in the neighbourhood and built a cell. Declan learned avidly with him and conceived a great desire to visit Rome. Here he spent some time, was consecrated by the Pope and, eventually, sent back to Ireland. It is said that on his journey home, Declan met St Patrick, who was travelling to Rome.

Declan had received from heaven a small black bell, subsequently known as *Duibhín Decláin* [Declan's little black thing]. When Declan and his followers sought to cross from Gaul to Britain no vessel could be found to transport them. The saint prayed to God and rang his bell. Immediately, an empty ship, without sails or sailors, put in to shore beside them. They embarked and were transported safely across the sea.

On preparing to cross to Ireland, one of Declan's followers, to whom the bell had been entrusted, inadvertently left it on a rock. Declan was much perturbed but, again, he prayed to God and the rock instantly floated out to sea and kept pace with the ship in which they were travelling. As they approached the Irish coast the rock was allowed to precede them and, therefore, effectively to choose the point at which they landed – on an island. This was taken to be the spot at which God had ordained that Declan should found his church. The local inhabitants resented Declan's having chosen to build on such an isolated spot and they hid his boats.

Declan prayed to God, struck the water with his staff and made the Sign of the Cross over it. The waters of the wide strait that separated the island from the mainland receded, leaving many fish behind on the deserted strand. This divinely reclaimed land proved to be most fertile, and by its fertility it helped to support the community of Declan's monastery at Ardmore.

In due course all the pre-Patrician missionaries, including Ibhar, who had been most opposed to Patrick, acknowledged him as their spiritual superior and so Declan was confirmed in his jurisdiction.

Shortly afterwards a great pestilence was raging in Munster as Declan was approaching Cashel. King Aengus entreated the saint to do something about it and, if possible, to restore life to the putrescent corpses. Declan prayed to God, the dead were restored to life and the pestilence died out throughout the whole area.

On another occasion a fleet of pagan pirates was observed approaching the shore. The people of the region rushed to Declan, now of advanced years, to seek miraculous salvation. Declan instructed his disciple Ultan to make a sign against the fleet, which Ultan did. Immediately all the vessels were swallowed by the sea, sinking 'as lead in the mighty waters'.

The site of Declan's monastery is marked by St Declan's Church, otherwise known as the Cathedral, a nave-and-chancel church with Romanesque arcading which is unique in Ireland; St Declan's Tomb or Oratory, which is said to contain the saint's grave and is a station of the annual pilgrimage held on his feast day, and a Round Tower, which is possibly the finest, and latest, in Ireland.

At the south end of the strand is a large stone, known as Declan's Stone, which is believed to be the rock which carried his bell, indicating to him the site of his monastery.

St Declan's Stone, Ardmore, Co. Waterford

25 July

NESSAN [NEASSAN]
of Mungret, Co. Limerick

Ruined church, Mungret, Co. Limerick

Nessan was a disciple of St Patrick's and was known as 'Nessan the Deacon'. He was also known as 'Nessan the Leper', presumably because he was, or had been, afflicted with the disease. He is reputed never to have told a lie. His monastery ranked among the greater abbeys and the learning of its monks was proverbial. He died in 551.

At one time there were said to be six churches and 1,600 religious in the monastery. All that remains now are two ruined churches.

31 July

NAAL [NADAL, NAEL, NOTAN, NADAN, NATALIS]
of Kilmanagh, Co. Kilkenny

Naal was born in the fifth century and is considered to be one of Patrick's disciples. At an early age he gave indications of great piety and, abandoning the pleasures of the world, embraced the religious life. He became the founder of the monastery at Kilmanagh [Church of the Monks], which soon acquired a reputation for learning and sanctity.

Church ruins, Kilmanagh, Co. Kilkenny

Among his pupils was Senan of Scattery Island and while on a journey with him, Naal observed a crowd of weeping and wailing persons. It transpired that the son of a local chieftain had just died and the mother of the deceased begged them on bended knee to restore him to life. Naal replied that this was beyond their powers, but when she insisted, with floods of tears, Naal instructed Senan to attempt the restoration. Despite modest protestations of his impotence, Senan embraced the dead body and persisted in his prayers until it was restored to life.

Naal died in 563. The only remaining relic of his once great monastery is Tobar Nadan [Nadan's Well]. A medieval wooden statue of the saint is preserved in St Kieran's College in Kilkenny.

UGUST

1 Colm; Failbhe; Miacca★; MO-RI; Nathi; RI-OG; RIOCH; Saran

2 Cobhran; Comhghan; Feichín; Lonán

3 Aodhán; DAIRBHILE★; DERIVLA★; DERVILL★; DERVILLA★; Cróchán; Feidhlimidh; Trea★

4 Berchan; LUA; LUGUID; Miodhnat; MOLUA

5 Colman; Duinseach★; Eirnín; Gormgall; Molioba; Ranait

6 Lughaidh; Mochua

7 Aodhán; Cillian; Cronan; Molacca; Senan; Tadg

8 Becan; Colman; Curcach★; Daire★

9 Barran★; Brecan; Ciarán; Colman; FEIDHLIMIDH; FELIM; Nathi; Ultan

10 Cuimín; Dachua; Malchus

11 ADROCHTA★; Aireran; ATHRACTA★; ATTRACTA★; Donnán; Liadhain★; Mianach; Talla★

12 Brighid; Iomhar; Lucan; LAISREN; MOLAISSE

13 Eimher; Lasairian; Mo-Maedoc; MUIREADHACH

14 Brogan; Caomhán; Cuimín; FACHTNA

15 Aodh; Colman; Saran

16 Conán; Lughan; Malcoisne

17 Beacán; Cormac; Earnán; Finnan; Seanán; Teimhen

18 Colman; DAIGH; DEGA; Eirnín; Odhrán; Ronana

19 Eanan; Ernán; MOCHTA

20 Cellach; Lasair*; Mothrenoch

21 Celba; Sionach; Uinchin

22 Barr; Beoghna; Cuimín; Sinche*

23 EUGENE; EOGHAN

24 Abban; Fachtna; Faolán; Seighin

25 Michen; Siollan

26 Aireid; Comhghall; Faolán

27 Aodhán; Usaille

28 Feidlimidh; Flannán

29 Finnen

30 Cronan; Fiachra; Loarn; Muadan

31 Aodh; Aodhán; Cillian; Cronan; Sessen

Church ruins, Inchbofin, Co. Longford

1 August

RIOCH [RI-OG, MO-RI]
of Inchbofin, Co. Longford

Rioch's father, Conis, is said to have been a Briton. The saint is described as a disciple of St Patrick's and is said to have served as his librarian. Although created a bishop by Patrick, Rioch was of a rather retiring nature and, through his humility, he distrusted his own abilities. Patrick therefore placed him on the island known as Inchbofin on Lough Ree, on the River Shannon, where he founded his monastery.

On one occasion in his island monastery he served up meat in a banquet for a visiting bishop, but unfortunately the bishop was unwilling to partake of flesh-meat. Then Rioch blessed the meat and it miraculously turned into bread, fish and honey.

Rioch died in 588. The site of his monastery is marked by two small churches: one is a small nave-and-chancel structure and the other has a nave with a Romanesque window. There are a few early grave-stones, three with inscriptions, and there are the remains of an enclosing cashel-wall.

3 August

DERVILLA [DERVILL, DERIVLA, DAIRBHILE]
of Fallmore, Co. Mayo

Dervilla was of noble family and her father was Cormac, a descendant of King

80

Dathi. She was a contemporary of St Columba's, founding her convent in the sixth century.

The site of her convent is marked by St Derivla's Church, a small primitive structure with a simple Romanesque west door with traces of badly eroded ornament, St Derivla's Bed or Grave with an early cross-slab, and Derivla's Vat, a holy well which is reputed to have curative powers.

4 August

MOLUA [LUA, LUGUID]
of Clonfertmulloe, Co. Laois

Molua was the youngest son of Carthach, or Coche, a prince of Munster, and his mother was Sochla. Even as a child he was capable of performing miracles, such as curing his father's cancerous foot and the ulcer of a man who cared for his parents' cattle.

On one occasion he and his friends were playing at making 'pretend-beer' from blackberry juice. However, since Molua was the 'chief brewer', the blackberry juice and water did become wine and all the children became intoxicated.

Molua became a student under Comgal of Bangor and performed a series of miracles there too – causing a paralytic to walk, because there was no horse to convey him, turning water into particularly sweet milk and producing very good flour from inferior grain.

When he left Bangor he set off in the direction of his home, until he reached the Slieve Bloom Mountains, on the southern slopes of which he founded the monastery to be known as Clonfertmulloe. Students flocked there and were received with tolerance and kindness. It was Molua's practice to deal leniently with his community and to achieve their spiritual correction, or improvement, only by mild persuasion and not with asperity of speech or manner.

A bard named Conan joined the community, but was unused to manual labour. Molua took him to a place where a great brake of thistles grew and on the first day they cut one, the next day two, the third day three, and so on, until ultimately a great clearing was made, thereby the bard was introduced gently to the rigours of labour in the fields.

The saint could, however, administer reproofs too, but in a fairly restrained fashion. On one occasion Brandubh, King of Leinster, arrived at Clonfertmulloe with 400 of his men and he asked that food be immediately prepared for all of them. Molua explained that it would be difficult to supply food for so many so speedily, but the king insisted, so Molua ordered food to be brought. The first morsel the king tasted stuck in his gullet and remained there for twenty-four hours, causing him great pain and preventing his eating, drinking or sleeping. He learned his lesson and on his recovery imparted many gifts to the community.

One day Molua observed a willow tree growing outside a monk's cell. Since he thought it would be much more agreeable for the monk, Molua turned it into an apple tree bearing fruit.

When he was advanced in years one of his teeth fell out and he instructed one of his monks to keep it carefully and not to bury it with him, since, in the future, it might become useful. Shortly after his death, between 605 and 615, some monks from abroad were touring Ireland, collecting relics of its saints. The community, understandably, was unwilling to disturb Molua's remains, but the tooth was duly produced as a relic of the holy man.

Of his monastery at Clonfertmulloe all that physically remains are a fragment of wall, St Molua's Grave, Trough and Stone. St Molua's Bell is preserved in the British Museum in London.

9 August

FELIM [FEIDHLIMIDH]
of Kilmore, Co. Cavan

Felim's mother, a grand-daughter of Dubtach úa Lugair, the chief poet of King Laoghaire, is said to have been married four times, and no fewer than six of her sons and one of her daughters became saints.

Felim is said to have been a monk at Slanore in Co. Cavan, under St Luthair, from which he moved to Kilmore, which was later to become the cathedral of the diocese to which it gave its name.

Of Felim's monastery nothing survives except the name, Kilmore, which means Big or Great Church; even the fine Romanesque doorway of the nineteenth-century Church of Ireland Cathedral is from a church on Trinity Island in Lough Oughter.

St Attracta's Well, Killaraght, Co. Sligo

11 August

ATTRACTA [ADROCHTA, ATHRACTA]
of Killaraght, Co. Sligo

Attracta's father was Talan, a native of Sligo. When she reached a suitable age her father sought to engage her in marriage but she, however, was intent on pursuing the religious life.

Accordingly she set off from home, with a maid called Mitain and a servant-man called Mochain, in search of St Patrick. She and her companion Mitain were both received into the religious life by Patrick. As he was consecrating them, a veil fell from heaven on Patrick's breast and he presented it to Attracta. Her modesty led her to demur and to suggest that her companion would be a more suitable recipient, which convinced Patrick that the veil was indeed intended for Attracta, and he placed it on her head.

Although she would have preferred a site near Drumconnell, where her brother Connell had a monastery, Patrick established a nunnery at the place later to be known as Killaraght, to which Attracta added a hospital, and he left her to rule over it, with some other pious women.

At the behest of King Bec, she destroyed a fearsome monster by thrusting a cross into its jaws. She restored to life a drowned bard; used deer instead of horses to draw a load of timber, and strands of her own hair, instead of rope, to tie the timber to the wagons.

Of her community the only physical remains are her cell, cross and well, at which stations were still performed within living memory.

St Attracta (Richard King, *Capuchin Annual*)

83

Wooden statue of St Laisren
(National Museum of Ireland)

12 August

LAISREN [MOLAISSE]
of Inishmurray, Co. Sligo

Mo-Laisse's House and the Saint's Bed,
Inishmurray, Co. Sligo

Laisren was a son of Declan and appears to have been trained at Candida Casa at Whithorn in Galloway, Scotland. He founded the monastery on the island of Inishmurray, which is, confusingly, named after St Muireadhach, first Bishop of Killala, who is supposed to be buried there. Laisren was a contemporary of both Patrick and Muireadhach, dying in the sixth century.

The monastic site is surrounded by a massive dry-stone rampart, divided into four sub-enclosures. In the largest of these is *Teach Mo-Laisse* [Mo-Laisse's House], a diminutive stone-roofed oratory containing a stone bench called *Leaba an Naoimh* [the Saint's Bed]. In the centre of the sub-enclosure is *Teampall Mo-Laisse* [Mo-Laisse's Church], apparently the principal monastic church. A third church, *Teampall Mhuire* [Mary's Church] stands outside the monastic enclosure.

There are numbers of inscribed early grave-slabs on the island, as well as the remains of stone-built monastic cells, and there is still an annual pilgrimage on Laisren's feast day.

A wooden statue of Laisren, which was found in the church, is now preserved in the National Museum in Dublin.

Round Tower at Killala, Co. Mayo

13 August

MUIREADHACH
of Killala, Co. Mayo

St Patrick founded a church at Killala and left Muireadhach, a member of his household, as its first bishop. It later became the cathedral of the diocese to which it gives its name. He is said to be buried on Inishmurray, Co. Sligo.

Of the monastic site at Killala the only ancient remnant is the fine Round Tower.

14 August

FACHTNA [FACHTNA MAC MONGAIGH]
of Ross Carbery, Co. Cork

St Muireadhach (Richard King,
Capuchin Annual)

Fachtna trained at Dairinis in Co. Cork, and he is said to have studied with both St Ita and St Finbar before founding his monastery at Ross Carbery, which was originally called Ros Ailithir [the Pilgrim's Promontory], after a pilgrim called Colman. The monastery became the principal establishment in Cork and was particularly famous for its school.

On one occasion he left an office-book at the spot on a hillside, about half a mile from the monastery, where he habitually went daily to pray. That night it rained very heavily, but the following day the book was bone-dry because the angels had built a small chapel over it.

Fachtna died in about 600 at the age of 46. Of the Priory of Our Lady, successor to the ancient monastery on the site, there are scant remains, but at Burgatia, a mile and a half to the east, is *Teampaillín Fhachtna* [Fachtna's Little Church] and Toberfaughtna, his well, to which pilgrims still come.

85

18 August

DAIGH [DEGA, DAIG MAC CAIRILL]
of Inishkeen, Co. Louth

Round Tower and church ruins,
Inishkeen, Co. Louth

Daigh's father was Cairell, a descendant of Niall of the Nine Hostages and his mother was Dechidu; he was a nephew of Molaisse of Devenish, Co. Fermanagh.

As a child he was placed under the care of Molaisse, who took him with him one day when he visited Mochta at his monastery in Louth. On meeting Daigh, Mochta predicted:

> Many a church vessel and ornament in gold, in silver, in brass and in iron, will proceed from that hand and many an elegant volume will it write.

And Daigh did become a celebrated craftsman.

He is said to have fashioned 150 bells and 100 croziers. He made cases or covers for sixty Gospel books. He made shrines, chalices, pyxes, dishes and crucifixes. He excelled as much in the writing of manuscripts, as he did in making covers for them.

After learning his crafts of writing and metal-working at his uncle's monastery, Daigh went to Bangor, where he worked for St Comgal. He then went to Clonmacnoise, famous for its workshops and scriptoria, where he worked for Kieran, until Kieran instructed him to found a monastery of his own. Accordingly he set off until he came to Inishkeen, where he founded his monastery. He died in 587.

The scant remains of the monastery include the stump of a Round Tower. Unfortunately we shall never know which, if any, of the bells and other ecclesiastical objects that survive were wrought by him.

Bronze ecclesiastical bell from
Lough Lene, Co. Kerry

19 August

MOCHTA
of Louth, Co. Louth

Mochta's parents were Britons and he was only an infant when they decided to leave their own country for Ireland. After receiving basic schooling – from an angel, it is said – he went to Rome where he furthered his education and received papal benediction before returning to Ireland.

He landed in Omeath but was not welcomed by the local people and was compelled to leave his first church. He then went to Louth, where he founded another one.

He came under the influence of Patrick and is described as Patrick's 'archipresbyter'. On founding his church at Louth he first laid out a cemetery and lit a fire. The local wizards recognised that unless they extinguished Mochta's fire, their own would be quenched. They tried pouring water on it, but the more water they poured, the bigger became the fire. Disciples flocked to him. From his monastery and school one hundred bishops and three hundred priests are said to have issued.

He performed many miracles. On one occasion, in the course of a journey, he and his companions were obliged to spend a night sleeping in the open. While they slept, their horses were stolen by robbers. Despite the thieves' travelling all night, the next morning they found themselves back with the saint and they were unable to dismount and escape. Mochta released them. They repented and joined his monastery. The saint died in 535 or 537.

St Mochta's House, a small stone-roofed church, is all that remains of his monastery, which at one time had grown to be one of the richest in Ireland.

23 August

EUGENE [EOGHAN]
of Ardstraw, Co. Tyrone

Eugene's father was called Cainnech, his mother Muindecha and Kevin of Glendalough was a close relative. He went to Clones where he studied with the youthful Tigernach. It was there that he and Tigernach were captured by pirates and carried off to Britain. They were both rescued and studied at Candida Casa at Whithorn in Galloway, Scotland, before returning to Ireland.

Eugene founded the monastery of Kilnamanagh [Church of the Monks] near Tallaght and here the youthful Kevin of Glendalough studied under him. Eugene then travelled North and established another monastery at Ardstraw, near the River Derg.

On one occasion a hundred captives of both sexes had been rounded up by pirates. They managed to get word to Eugene, who passed unseen through the pirate camp, baptised the captives and spirited all of them away.

Of his monastery at Ardstraw not a single trace survives.

EPTEMBER

1 Cuimín; Failbhe; Nemen; Sceallan

2 Colm; Eanan; Mainne; Molotha★; Seanán

3 AENGUS; CAEMHAN; CAEMAN BREAC; Colman; MAC NISSI

4 Aodhán; Comhghall; Cuimín; Failbhe; Fiachra; Seanán; Serbhile★; ULTAN

5 Eolog; Faelan; Olan

6 Bega; Caenchomhrac; Colm; Colman; Coinnait; Sciath★

7 Siollan; Toit; Ultan

8 Fearghus; Fionntán; Maelcoisne

9 Cera★; CIARÁN; Conall; Fionnbharr; KIERAN; Osmana★

10 Ailbhe; Fearghus; FINNIAN; Fionnbharr; Odhrán; Segen

11 Colman; Conmael; Dónal; Loarn; Siollan

12 AILBE; AILBHE; ALBY; Colman; Fleid★; LAISRE; LASREN; MO-LAISSE

13 Ailbhe; Dagan; Maeltolaigh; Naomhán

14 Caomhán; Cormac

15 Ainmire; Lassair

16 Caomhán; Colman; Criotan; Lasairian; Seanán

17 Cuimín; Fema⋆; Grellan; Riaghail

18 Enan; Eoain; Meno

19 Ainchi; Caoimgell; Fionntán

20 Aodhán; Moghaidh

21 Saran

22 Ailioll; Aodh; Barrfin; Colm; Colman

23 ADOMNAN; ADHAMHNÁN; Comnat⋆; EUNAN; Tecla⋆

24 Ceallachán; Coalchu

25 BAIRRE; Caolán; Colman; FIONNBARR; FINBAR; LOCHAN; Seanán

26 Colman

27 Finnian

28 Diarmaid; Fiachra; Machan; Sinach mac Dara

29 Ciarán; Colm; Colman; Comhghall; Murgal; Neasan

30 Airmne; Brighid⋆; Colman; Conna; Faolán; Lughaidh; Seanán

Kells Abbey, Co. Antrim

3 September

MAC NISSI [AENGUS, CAEMHAN, CAEMAN BREAC]
of Connor, Co. Antrim

Mac Nissi's father was Fobrec, his mother Cnes, but it was his mother's name that he bore [*mac* Cneise, son of Cnes]. His birth was foretold by Patrick and he was put into the care of St Olcan, as his foster-child. He was baptised by Patrick, educated by St Olcan and it was Patrick who consecrated him bishop.

As a child the saint fell asleep while supposed to be tending cows and their young calves and for this his mother beat him. Her hand became paralysed until he prayed for her, when it was immediately restored. He used to carry his master's books in a leather satchel.

He made a pilgrimage, not only to Rome, but to Jerusalem as well, from which he brought back 'a stone from our Lord's sepulture, a lock of the hair of the Blessed Virgin Mary, a bone of the Apostle Thomas, portions of garments belonging to the Apostles and one of the bowls belonging to the Great Altar at Jerusalem'.

Returning by Rome, he was accorded the honour of consecrating and ordaining bishops, priests and deacons. Before he left, in recognition of the poverty of the Irish Mission, he was presented with gifts of gold, silver and brass vessels.

Mac Nissi was gifted with miraculous powers. Two men, one blind, the other a leper, were cured by washing in a fountain of pure water, accompanied by the saint's prayers. On another occasion he saved the life of a youth called Colman: he was about to be executed by being thrown into the air so that he would land on the spears of his executioners. Instead, he landed safely in the arms of the saint.

Mac Nissi travelled in Munster with Patrick and Brigid and passing the spot – later to be known as Lynally [*Lan Elo*, the Church of Colman Elo] – he had a vision of the heavens opening and the angels of God descending and ascending. On that same day he predicted the birth of Colman Elo sixty years hence and the foundation of a monastery on that spot by him. He also predicted the birth of Comgal of Bangor.

Through Mac Nissi's intercession a woman of advanced years, who had not had a child for fifteen years, was able to bring forth a son.

Mac Nissi founded a church at Connor, a place described as being 'an oakwood wherein wolves used to be formerly', about 480. He also established a hermitage at Kells, which was later to become an important monastery. Here, according to one of his 'Lives', he is said to have

> commanded a river that flowed past the monastery to flow by a more distant course, lest the sound of it as it passed might be hurtful to the sick of the place.

St Mac Nissi died between 506 and 514. The only material relic of the foundation at Connor is a fragment of a High Cross. The name of the monastery, of course, is remembered as the name of the diocese and the name of its founder as the diocesan patron.

4 September

ULTAN [ULTAN MOCCU CONCHOBAIR]
of Ardbraccan, Co Meath

Ultan was a relative of St Brigid of Kildare. He became abbot and bishop of the monastery founded at Ardbraccan by St Braccan – another name for the monastery was *Tiobraid Ultáin* [Ultan's Well]. He is said to have 'fed with his own hands every child in Erin who had no support', and he provided particular care for the children of women who were carried off by a plague. He had a reputation for austerity: he used to bathe in cold water regardless of the biting wind.

He is the first person known to have concerned himself with recording the acts of St Patrick [Tirechan, author of a *Life of St Patrick*, was a disciple of Ultan's]. Several literary works, including a skilful and elaborate poem, *Brigid Bé*, in honour of St Brigid, have been ascribed to him. He died between 656 and 663.

The only physical relic of the monastery where he worked is *Tiobraid Ultáin*.

Ruins of the monastery at Clonmacnoise,
Co. Offaly

9 September

KIERAN [CIARÁN]
of Clonmacnoise, Co. Offaly

Cross of the Scriptures, Clonmacnoise,
Co. Offaly (Commissioners of Public
Works in Ireland)

Kieran was born near Fuerty, Co. Roscommon, in Connacht; his father was a chariot-builder by trade and a native of the north-east who had settled in Connacht.

Kieran was a disciple of St Finnian of Clonard. While Kieran was at Clonard Ninnidh of Inishmacsaint asked him for the loan of a book. It so happened that Kieran had just reached the point in Matthew's Gospel where it says, 'Do unto others as you would be done by.' Kieran laughed and lent him the book.

After Kieran founded a monastery on Inis Ainghin, now known as Hare Island, in Lough Ree, he travelled down the River Shannon with eight companions on 25 February 547 to found the monastery of Clonmacnoise. There is a legend that Diarmaid I, King of Tara, helped Kieran with his own hands to build the first wooden church at Clonmacnoise. Seven months after the monastery was built, on 9 September 549, Kieran died.

When he first arrived at Clonmacnoise he had said:

Here shall I dwell, in this place many souls will go to the Kingdom of God, and in this place shall my resurrection be.

He is said never to have looked upon a woman in his life and never to have told a lie.

His church, later a large monastery, or even a monastic city, with twelve or thirteen churches or oratories, became the chief monastery of Connacht, despite its being on the east, or Leinster, side of the Shannon. In the whole of

Ireland, Clonmacnoise was second only to Armagh as an ecclesiastical centre, while as a centre of Irish art and literature, it probably had no rival.

The surviving products of its scriptoria include some of the most important Irish manuscripts: *Leabhar na hUidre* [The Book of the Dun Cow]; *Chronicon Scotorum* [The Chronicle of the Irish]; *Annals of Clonmacnoise*; *Annals of Tigernach*.

The products of its workshops include some of the greatest masterpieces of Irish metalwork: St Kieran's Crozier, The Crozier of the Abbots of Clonmacnoise, the Cross of Cong, St Manchan's Shrine.

The buildings on the site today are formidable, even though they represent only a fraction of what was once there. In 1197 no fewer than 105 houses were burned down and its former magnificence was finally reduced to a complete ruin by the English in 1552, when 'not a bell, large or small, or an image, or an altar, or a book, or a gem, or even glass in a window, was left which was not carried away'. While not a single workshop or dwelling survives, there still remain eight churches, including the diminutive Temple Kieran, traditionally the burial-place of the saint. There is a good Round Tower with a Romanesque doorway; a group of three High Crosses, including the Cross of the Scriptures. There is, too, a spectacular collection of inscribed early grave-slabs.

Inscribed graveslab, Clonmacnoise, Co. Offaly (Commissioners of Public Works in Ireland)

10 September

FINNIAN [FINNIAN MOCCU FIATACH]
of Movilla, Co. Down

Finnian's parents were Christians. His father was Corpre and his mother Lassara. He studied at Candida Casa at Whithorn in Galloway, Scotland, like many of the early Irish churchmen. He went to Rome and it was he who introduced the Vulgate to Ireland.

In about 540 he founded his monastery at the head of Strangford Lough. His reputation for scholarship and his monastery, together with its school, attracted many pupils, including Columba. It was here that Columba copied a manuscript of Finnian's and Finnian claimed the copy as his. Columba disputed this. The disagreement over the copyright went for arbitration to the High King, who produced the famous judgement: 'To every cow its calf, to every book its copy.'

Before Finnian died in 579 he was confined to bed for twelve months. On one occasion he restored to life a widow's son who had been dead for three days. Monks of his school seem to have been involved in the origination of the famous *Lebor Gabála Érenn* [The Book of the Taking of Ireland].

The only physical evidence of the site of the monastery is an early inscribed grave-slab and the ruins of a thirteenth- to fifteenth-century church.

Round Tower and churches, Devenish, Co. Fermanagh

12 September

MOLAISSE [MO-LAISSE, LAISRE, LASREN]
of Devenish, Co. Fermanagh

Molaisse's father was Natfraich and his mother Monua. He studied under Finnian of Clonard and, while there, he was one day sitting with Mogue of Ferns in the shade of trees. They were debating what they should do, and eventually sought divine guidance on whether or not they should work together or separately. The tree under which Mogue was sitting fell, and pointed South. Molaisse's tree fell and pointed North. They recognised the meaning and tearfully bade each other farewell. Molaisse went North to found his monastery on Devenish in Lough Erne. He is said to have made a pilgrimage to Rome and to have brought several relics back to Ireland with him.

There is a nice story that once, when he was on a journey in Ireland, he met a group of monks who had a rather good map. He was anxious to copy it, but discovered he had no pen with him. An obliging goose flying overhead dropped a quill into his hand, thus enabling him to make his copy.

94

He died in 564 or 571. The remains of the monastic site include two churches, one known as Mo-Laisse's House, a small stone-roofed Romanesque oratory which was still intact in the eighteenth century, and a larger one known as Mo-Laisse's Church. There is a good Round Tower and the foundations only of a second. Farther up the hill, nearer the centre of the island, are the remains of the fifteenth-century St Mary's Abbey. The eleventh-century reliquary, *Soiscéal* [Gospel] *Mo-Laisse*, known as the Satchel of Molaisse, now preserved in the National Museum in Dublin, belonged to this monastery.

12 September

ALBY [AILBE, AILBHE]
of Emly, Co. Tipperary

Alby was another of the pre-Patrician missionaries. It is said that his father was Olcnais and his mother Sandith, a maid-servant of a chief called Cronan.

Cronan was greatly displeased at the birth of a child to his maid-servant and ordered that the child be exposed to dogs and wild beasts that it might be devoured. But the saint was rescued by a group of Britons who were living in Ireland; though another story has it that he was rescued and reared by a wolf, to which he was able to give sanctuary in later life.

He subsequently made his way to Rome where he was consecrated a bishop by the Pope. On his return he joined Colman and instructed him to build a church in Kilroot in Dalaradia [Dál nAraide]. He restored to life the three sons of King Fintan, who had been waging war with Connacht and losing. The following year, after the king had been blessed by Alby, he was victorious.

Alby was described as 'that other Patrick of the island of Ireland'. He met Patrick at Cashel and acknowledged him as his religious superior.

Alby seems to have chosen the site of a pagan sanctuary for his church at Emly – a sanctuary coincidentally associated with a mythical Ailbhe. The monastery he founded was to become one of the greatest and wealthiest in Munster, and it gave its name to a diocese. There is good reason to suppose that the major part of the *Annals of Inisfallen* were compiled in this monastery. It was Alby who obtained permission for St Enda to establish his monastery on Inishmore. Alby died in 527.

The Church of Ireland parish church at Emly occupies the site of the monastery and in the churchyard is a crude stone cross, and St Alby's Well, which is still visited on the saint's day.

23 September

EUNAN [ADOMNAN, ADHAMHNÁN]
of Raphoe, Co Donegal

Eunan was a native of Raphoe, his father was Ronan and his mother Ronnat. He was born in 624 and he seems to have entered the monastery, founded locally in the sixth century by Colmcille, before going to Iona.

While he was there, he was engaged with his monks in drawing timbers over the sea with a flotilla of currachs, for a building at the monastery. Suddenly the wind whipped up – timbers, currachs, monks and even Eunan himself were all in deadly peril – but Eunan prayed to God and the wind was assuaged. On his return to Ireland he is said to have founded many monasteries before returning to Iona in 678, where he served as Abbot from 679 until his death in 704.

While working in Ireland he was instrumental in securing the release of sixty captives taken from Meath by Saxon raiders. He went to meet King Aldfrith to negotiate the release of the prisoners. When Eunan and his companions hauled their ships onto the shore Eunan drew a circle round them and the place where the ships lay became an island. The Saxons, observing this keenly, trembled in fear. Eunan's negotiations were totally successful. His two requests – the release of the captives and a cessation of the raids – were granted.

At a Convention or *Mórdháil*, Eunan's proposal that woman be excluded from future warfare was nationally accepted.

He is said to have had a knowledge of Hebrew and Greek, as well as being fluent in Latin. He is best known for his *Vita Sancti Columbae* [Life of St Columba], which is an account of the life and works of the great Irish saint and founder of so many Irish monasteries. It is a superb work and casts a great deal of light on many aspects of the early Irish Church. As Eunan himself says of it:

> Let no one suppose that I will write concerning this so memorable man either falsehood or things that might be doubtful or unsure, but let him understand that I shall relate what has come to my knowledge through the tradition passed on by our predecessors and by trustworthy men who knew the facts.

All that remains of the early monastery at Raphoe are fragments of two pre-Romanesque door lintels. The Round Tower was demolished in about 1660 by the Protestant Bishop, John Lesley, to provide building material for his palace.

Raphoe gave its name to a diocese and Eunan is its patron.

25 September

FINBAR [FIONNBARR, BAIRRE, LOCHAN]
of Cork, Co. Cork

Oratory at Gougane Barra, Co. Cork

Finbar is said to have been the son of a metal-worker called Amergin and to have been born at Rath Raithlenn in Co. Cork, which has been identified with the excavated earthen fort, Lisnacaheragh, near Garranes, Co. Cork, where, indeed, there was abundant evidence of metal-working about 500.

The saint was taken off, with his parents' permission, by a group of anchorites (hermits) from Leinster. He first went to Aghaboe, Co. Laois, but Canice asked him to leave, since it had been destined for Canice's charge.

After he left Aghaboe he was met by King Fachtna 'The Angry', who brought with him a blind son and a mute daughter. Finbar blessed them and they were immediately healed. Later he met the king again and, while they were talking, they heard a wail. King Fachtna interpreted this as meaning his infirm wife had just died. Finbar blessed some water and told Fachtna to wash his dead wife in it. She returned to life forthwith and in gratitude the king offered the saint a tract of land.

On another occasion, as a display of divine power, he caused nuts to appear on a tree in spring. He founded a monastery at Gougane Barra, near the source of the River Lee, before travelling downstream to found another monastery, where the angel of God had indicated, on the south bank of the river, on the hill-slope south-west of the present city of Cork.

His consecration as a bishop took place in a miraculous fashion. He and his teacher, Meccuirp, were raised up by the angels of the Lord and consecrated and then let down by the altar. Oil broke forth from the earth near the altar and covered the feet of those standing there.

He died at Cloyne, probably in 623, and his body was translated to Cork to be deposited in a silver shrine. His monastery grew in significance and became head of an important confederation of south Munster monastic churches. It was the setting for the twelfth-century *Visio Tungdali*, an Irish contribution to medieval vision-literature which was translated into six European languages.

The foundations of the Church of Ireland Cathedral were laid in 1867 on the site of Finbar's monastery where the stump of a Round Tower had stood. Of the monastery, all that now remains is a collection of Romanesque fragments preserved in the chapter house of the Cathedral. At Gougane Barra, however, on a small island in the lake, there is a little oratory and the remains of cells, which pilgrims still visit on the Sunday after St Finbar's feast day.

St Finbar (Ruth Brandt and Colin Smythe Limited)

CTOBER

1 Clothra★; Colm; Colman; Fionntán; Loigteach
2 Giallan; Liadhnan; Mobhi; ODHRÁN; ORAN
3 Moidelbh; Nuada; Tearnoch
4 Bigseach; Colman; Fionán; Seanán
5 Baothghalach; Forthach; Sinech★
6 Aodh; Baoithin; Colman; Lughaidh
7 Ceallach; Comhghall; Colman; Dubhthach
8 Ciarán; Corcran; Maelcritiog
9 Aodhán; Dinertach; Fionntán
10 Fionntán; Seanán; Siollan★
11 CAINNEACH; CANICE; Fortchern; LOMÁN; LOMMAN
12 BERCHAN; CLÁRAINECH; Diarmaid; Faolán; FIACC; FIACH; MO-BI
13 Ciar★; Colman; Comhghan; Findsech★
14 Colm
15 Colman; Cormac; Cuan; Galma★
16 Caoimhghin; Caomhán; Ciar; Colm; COLMAN; Eoghan; Gall

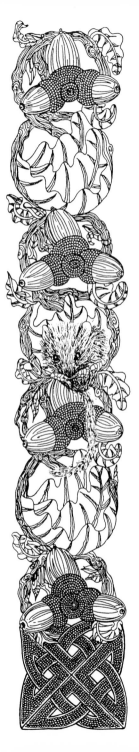

17 Maonach

18 Colman; Lonán; Teca★

19 Colman; Cronan; Faolán

20 Aodhán; Colman; Fionntán

21 FINTAN; FIONNTÁN; Mainchín; MO-FHINNU; MUNNU

22 Cillian; Donnchadh

23 Cillian; Dalbhac

24 Colman; Lonán; Tadhg

25 Caoide; Conac★; Gorman; Lasairian

26 Beoan; Caol★; Derbhile★; Earnan; Odhrán

27 Abbán; Colman; Earnán; Odhrán

28 Colman; Cronan; Suibhne

29 Aodh; Caolán; Colman; Cuan; Luran; Taimhthionna★

30 Colman; Ercnat★; Feidhlimidh

31 Colman; Comán; Faolán

2 October

ORAN [ODHRÁN]
of Latteragh, Co. Tipperary

Oran and his brother Medran went to St Kieran at Seir Kieran; Medran decided to stay there, while Oran – to whom the title 'Magister' or 'Master' was applied – was sent to build and to become the first abbot of a new foundation at Latteragh. He died in 548.

The only ecclesiastical remains on the site are the ruins of a twelfth-century church.

Church at Latteragh, Co. Tipperary

11 October

CANICE [CAINNEACH]
of Aghaboe, Co. Laois

Despite his being better known as the founder of a church at, and as patron of, Kilkenny, to which he gave his name, Canice's major foundation was at Aghaboe. Indeed there is no historical mention of the church at Kilkenny until 1085. He was a contemporary and friend of Columba's. There is a nice story that Columba was out in a boat with some monks when they were caught in a storm. The terrified monks begged Columba to pray for their safety, but Columba simply kept on rowing and said that on this occasion he would leave the praying to Canice.

Canice, meanwhile, was just about to sit down to a meal in his monastery at Aghaboe when he suddenly jumped up and ran to the church so quickly that he

St Canice's Cathedral, Kilkenny,
Co. Kilkenny

lost a shoe in his haste. As soon as he started his prayer the storm abated and Columba turned to his companions and said:

> The Lord has listened to Canice's prayer, and his race to the church with one shoe has saved us.

Canice died at Aghaboe in 600. A church was built there as a shrine for the saint in 1052, only to be destroyed, together with his relics, in 1346. Nothing now remains of the original foundation.

At Kilkenny the only surviving fragment of the early monastic site is the Round Tower. Nearby, however, is St Kenny's Well.

11 October

LOMÁN [LOMMAN]
of Trim, Co. Meath

According to ancient tradition the lord of the district, Felim, son of King

St Lomán (Brigid Rynne and The Talbot Press)

Laoghaire of Tara, presented 'his territory with all his goods and all his race' to Lomán and St Patrick. Patrick built a church at Trim and Lomán, a British disciple of Patrick's, was appointed its first bishop. Lomán's successors served as bishops and abbots and, for generations, they were chosen exclusively from Felim's descendants.

The site of the early monastery, of which nothing remains, is marked by St Mary's Abbey with its magnificent fourteenth-century bell-tower.

12 October

FIACH [FIACC]
of Sleaty, Co. Laois

St Patrick founded a church at Sleaty and ordained Fiach as its bishop, leaving seven of his own household with him. Fiach's first monastery was on the east side of the River Barrow, at a spot called *Domhnach Féic* [Fiach's Church]. After sixty of his monks fell ill an angel visited him and warned him to move the site of the monastery to the western side of the river.

The scant remains include two tall, but undecorated, granite crosses and the ruins of a medieval church.

12 October

BERCHAN [CLÁRAINECH, MO-BI, MO-BHI]
of Glasnevin, Co. Dublin

Berchan founded a monastery at Glasnevin on the banks of the River Tolka. His nick-name, *Clárainech*, is distinctly unflattering – meaning 'flat-faced'. The monastic church was on the eastern bank of the river and the monks' dwellings on the western one. The school attached to the monastery was famous and numbered among its pupils Columba and Canice. Its success was short-lived, however, as it was wiped out by a plague, in which Berchan died in 545.

No trace of the monastery survives, though the Church of Ireland parish church may occupy part of the site.

16 October

COLMAN
of Kilroot, Co. Antrim

Colman built a church at Kilroot in 512 at the bidding of St Alby of Emly. Since the place had no water St Alby blessed a stone and from it burst forth a stream. When Colman complained that the water-supply was poor, Alby replied: 'Though it is small it will never fail, and the stream will continue for ever, to the end of the world.'

There are rather scanty remains of a church at the site.

Cross from a slab at Kilroot, Co. Antrim

21 October

FINTAN [FIONNTÁN MOCCU MOIE, MO-FHINNU, MUNNU]
of Taghmon, Co. Wexford

Fintan was the son of a Druid called Tailchán or Tulchán. As a youth he was charged with tending his father's flocks, but came under the influence of a hermit who taught him to read and fostered his interest in the church.

His father feared that the care of his flocks might be suffering and watched one night to see if this was so. To his amazement two wolves came to guard the sheep while the lad pursued his studies with the hermit.

Fintan joined St Comgal's monastery at Bangor and then went to Iona, but by the time he arrived there, Columba was already dead and had left instructions that Fintan was to return to Ireland and found a monastery of his own.

The saint founded one at Taughmon, Co. Westmeath, as well as another with the same name, *Teach Munnu* [Munnu's House], at Taghmon, in Co. Wexford. At a synod held about 630 to discuss the date of Easter, Fintan was the principal spokesman for the traditionalists against the modernists led by Laisren of Leighlin. St Fintan died in 635.

At the Wexford site only a well, *Tobar Munna*, and fragments of a cross survive. The site of the Westmeath monastery is occupied by a fifteenth-century church.

OVEMBER

1 Ailltin★; Aodh; Breannain; Cairbre; Caoimhe★; Colman; Cronan; Lonán

2 Ainmire; Aodhán; Caoimhe★; EARC; ERC; Lughaidh

3 Caomhán; Conodhar; MALACHY; MAOLMAEDHOG; Muiredheabhar

4 Tiarnach

5 Colman; Faolán; Flannán

6 Aodhán; Cronan; Fedhbar★

7 Colman; Fionntán

8 Barrfionn; Colm

9 Aodhnait★; BEANNAN; BENEN; BENIGNUS; Fionntán; MIONNAN; Sineach★

10 AEDH; AODH; Ciarán; Comán; Fearghus; Osnat★

11 Cairbre; Cronan; Dubhan; Maolodhrain; Sinel

12 Cuimín; Eirnín; Lonán; Mainchín

13 Eirnín; Lorcán; Nainnid; Odharnait★

14 Colman; Lorcán

15 Connait

2 November

ERC [EARC]
of Slane, Co. Meath

St Patrick is said to have lit his first Paschal fire in Ireland at Slane, on the hill. Down by the River Boyne he established a church over which he placed Erc as bishop, a man credited with the practice of great austerities. Despite the relics of Erc having been taken to Teltown in 776, the Round Tower at Slane, together with 'the best of bells' and the enshrined crozier of Erc, was destroyed by Vikings in 948.

In the graveyard of the 'abbey' are the two gable-ends of an early stone shrine-shaped tomb which is all that remains of the early monastery.

3 November

MALACHY [MAOLMAEDHOG O'MORGAIR]
of Armagh, Co. Armagh

Arms of the archdiocese of Armagh

Malachy, or Maolmaedhog as he was then called, was born in 1094 or 1095, at Armagh, the son of Mughron O'Morgair, and his mother was an O'Hanratty. When Malachy was eight years old his father died and he was placed under the care of Imhar Ó hAodhagáin. He was ordained as a priest at the age of twenty-five by Archbishop Ceallach, for whom he had acted as vicar from 1119 to 1121.

After training at Lismore in Co. Waterford – then the monastery with the closest links to Britain and the continent – he was appointed Bishop of Down and Connor in 1124 and went to Bangor, Co. Down. It was at this stage, it is said, that he assumed the biblical name of Malachy. His biographer St Bernard records that when he went at first to Down and Connor:

> Never had he known men so steeped in barbarism, nowhere had he found people so wanton in their way of life, so cruel in superstition, so heedless of Faith, lawless, unbending in the face of discipline, so vile in their life-style. They were Christians in name but pagans in reality.

In the face of this situation he was spurred to become one of the great reformers of the Church in Ireland.

In 1127, Bangor was overrun by a Mac Lochlainn, King of Cenél Eoghain, and Malachy and his monks were forced to flee to Munster.

When Malachy left the diocese Bernard was able to report:

> Their hardness of heart yielded, their barbarity was quelled, the disobedient house began to be relaxed little by little. Barbarous customs were abolished and those of Rome introduced.

Malachy's journeys to Rome, as representative of the Irish bishops, brought him into contact with St Bernard of Clairvaux. In 1129 he was nominated successor to Ceallach as Bishop of Armagh and was sent his crozier as a token. Despite the opposition of Clann Sinaigh, who regarded themselves as having a hereditary right to the see, he eventually occupied the throne, but in 1137 he retired to the newly separated bishopric of Down, which he established at the site of Comgal's old monastery at Bangor; from there he continued his efforts to reform the Irish Church.

In 1148, with the assistance of Bernard of Clairvaux, with whom he had had friendly contact for years, he had introduced the Cistercian Order to Ireland, with its first abbey at Mellifont, Co. Louth. Soon the number of Cistercian houses in Ireland numbered thirty.

Malachy died in 1148 at Clairvaux. In 1190 he was canonised by Pope Clement III and soon after some of the saint's relics were brought from Clairvaux to Mellifont and other Irish Cistercian houses.

Cistercian Abbey at Mellifont, Co. Louth
(Commissioners of Public Works
in Ireland)

9 November

BENEN [BEANNAN, BENIGNUS, MIONNAN]
of Kilbennan, Co. Galway

Benen's father was Sesegne and when Benen was very young – a toddler, in fact – Patrick came to his father's home and won all to the faith. Benen followed Patrick wherever he went, brought him flowers when he rested, much to the embarrassment of his family which tried to hold him back.

'Restrain him not,' said St Patrick. 'That child shall inherit my Kingdom.'

When the time came for Patrick to go, Benen refused to leave him, locking his legs round the saint's knee, so Sesegne gave him into Patrick's keeping.

107

From boyhood, therefore, he accompanied Patrick on his mission, serving later as his psalm-singer, or choir-master. He was ordained a priest and founded a church at what was to become Kilbennan, in Galway, at which St Jarlath of Tuam was a student. He also appears to have founded a small church on Inishmore in the Aran Islands.

According to some traditions he became Patrick's favourite disciple, and certainly became his successor as Patrick had predicted, becoming second Bishop of Armagh. A medieval tale tells of how Patrick and Benen called forth a spring by lifting the sod. The two of them are said to have healed and baptised nine lepers there. Benen died in 467.

Of his foundation at Kilbennan a ruined Round Tower and a fragmentary church survive, and also a well, which was the scene of a great *pátrún* [festivities on a feast day] until the mid-nineteenth century. On Inishmore there is a small structure, with trabeate doorway, known as Teampall Mionnáin, or Temple Benen, some cells and the remains of an enclosing wall.

10 November

AEDH [AODH MAC BRIC, HUGH]
of Rahugh, Co. Westmeath

Aedh was said to be a northerner from Donegal. He founded his church in Rahugh, Co. Westmeath, in the sixth century. He was also connected with a hermitage on Slieve League in Co. Donegal, which was associated with St Assicus of Elphin in Co. Roscommon.

At Rahugh are St Hugh's Well, and St Hugh's Tombstone, a fine early cross-slab reputed to cure headaches. On Slieve League are the remains of the oratory and well of St Aodh mac Bric, to which there is still a pilgrimage.

Aodh mac Bric's Oratory, Slieve League,
Co. Donegal

18 November

RONAN
of Dromiskin, Co. Louth

A church was founded at Dromiskin by St Patrick over which he placed two members of his household, Do-Lue and Lugaid, sons of Aengus, King of Cashel. Its most celebrated abbot was Ronan, who died in 664.

His relics were placed in a costly shrine in 801 and were long venerated here, presumably until it was occupied by the Vikings for some years in the tenth century. The only remnants of the early monastery are the Round Tower and St Ronan's Well.

24 November

COLMAN [COLMAN MAC LENENE]
of Cloyne, Co. Cork

Colman was a native of Muskerry, Co. Cork, and is said to have been a professional poet before entering the Church, which he was induced to do in his later years by St Brendan.

Churches with his name are common in mid-Cork. He founded the church of Kilmaclenine, near Kilcolman, in Co. Cork. The site at Cloyne was given to him by Cairpre Crom, King of Cashel. He is the earliest known Irish poet to have made use of Latin rhymes, though only fragments of his work have survived.

At Kilmaclenine are some ruinous fragments of the early church, while at Cloyne the only surviving relic is the Round Tower whose roof was damaged – and botchily repaired – in 1748.

25 November

FINCHU [FIONNCHU, FINDCHU]
of Brigown, Co. Cork

The monastery at Brigown was actually founded by St Abban but Finchu was a bishop there.

He was a man of remarkable asceticism. There is a story that he surrendered his assured place in heaven to a king of the Deisi and to win a new place for himself he mortified his flesh with seven sickles made by seven smiths.

Finchu died of the Yellow Plague in 664. There was a Round Tower at Brigown until it fell in 1720 and there is now only a graveyard with sparse remains of a church.

ECEMBER

1 Bréanainn; Neaśan

2 Cuimín; Mainchín; Maolodhran

3 Colman; Maccoige

4 Bearchán; Mainchín; Suairleach

5 Colman; Seanán

6 Breaccan; GOBAN FIONN; GOBBAN; Meallan; Neasán

7 BUIN; BUITE; BUITHIN; Colman; Ollan

8 Bréanainn; Fionán

9 Feidelm★

10 Colman; Modimog; Senach

11 Colm; Meltog

12 Colman; FINIAN; FINNIAN; FINNIO; Flannán

13 Baedan; Bréanainn; COLM; COLMAN; COLUM; Cormac

14 Colman; Cormac; Dallan; Eirnín; Fionntán

15 Colman; Cronan; Flann; Moghain★

16 Mobheoc; Rodaighe

17 Crunmaol; Senchadh

18 Caomhán; Colman; Cuimín; Éimhín; Flannán; Lioban★; Maighnenn; Rioghnach★; Seanán

19 Commaigh★; SAFAN★; SAMHTHANN★

20 Diarmaid; Eoghan; Feidhlimidh; Fraoch

21 Flann; Siollan

22 ÉIMHÍN; EMIN; EVIN; Tua; Ultan

23 Colman; Éirnín; Feidhlimidh; Ronan

24 Cuimín; Maolmhuire; Mochua; Seanán

25 Aodhán; Maolan

26 COMÁN; COMMAN; Iarfhlaith; Lasairian; Mogenog; Moliba

27 Colman; Fiacha; Tiobrat

28 Cillian; Feichín; Muireadhach

29 Aileran; Éanán; Fionnán; Mainchín

30 Ailbhe; Connla

31 Éanna; Lochan

High Cross, Killamery, Co. Kilkenny
(Commissioners of Public Works
in Ireland)

6 December

GOBBAN [GOBAN FIONN]
of Killamery, Co. Kilkenny

Gobban left Leighlin to St Laisren, apparently founded Seagoe in Co. Armagh, and then came to Killamery, where he is said to have ruled over 1,000 monks. He died in 639 and is buried at Clonenagh in Co. Laois.

The only relics of his monastery are a fine eighth-century High Cross, an early gravestone and a well, *Tobar Naoimh Niocláis* [St Nicholas's Well].

7 December

BUITE [BUITHIN, BUIN]
of Monasterboice, Co. Louth

Buite was the son of Bronach. He went to Rome and returned to Ireland by way of Scotland, where he restored Nectan, King of the Picts, to life. He founded monasteries in Scotland, including Kirkbuddo [Church of Buite].

On his return to Ireland he founded a monastery at Monasterboice in the Boyne Valley, which was to become one of the chief abbeys and centres of learning in the country. He died in 521.

In 1097 the Round Tower there was damaged by fire and books and other treasures were destroyed. The remains on the site consist of two simple churches, two early grave-slabs, the Round Tower and three High Crosses; one is *Cros Bhuithín* [St Buite's Cross], covered overall with carved panels; another is known as Muiredach's Cross, because of the inscription on the base which commemorates the fact that Muiredach erected it; the third, the North Cross, is fairly plain apart from a crucifixion on the west face.

The Arrest of Christ from Muiredach's
Cross, Monasterboice, Co. Louth
(Commissioners of Public Works
in Ireland)

12 December

FINNIAN [FINIAN, FINNIO MOCCU TELDUIB]
of Clonard, Co. Meath

Finnian's father was Finntan and his mother Telach. During his mother's pregnancy, a flame came into her mouth and came out of it in the form of a bright bird. The bird sat on the branch of a tree and was joined by 'all the birds and bird-flights' of the south of Ireland. Then it went to the North and sat in the branch of another tree and was joined by 'all the birds and bird-flights' of the whole of Ireland, which was interpreted as a portent of how saintly the infant was to become.

He was baptised by Abban and founded three churches in his youth. At the age of thirty he went overseas, to Tours; he then wanted to go to Rome but an angel came to him and said: 'What would be given to you in Rome will be given to you here.'

He returned to Ireland where he founded a monastery at Aghowle in Co. Wicklow. Here he stayed for some years attracting many disciples.

He then went on to a place called Aghafeacle, where one of his teeth fell out and he hid it in a brake of brambles. When he was preparing to leave this place the members of his community asked him to leave a sign with them. He told them to go into the brake and to bring out the tooth that was there. They went to the brake, which had burst into flames, and retrieved the tooth.

He went to visit Brigid at Kildare, who gave him a gold ring when he was leaving. He declined the ring, but Brigid insisted, saying he would need it. Shortly after, he met Caisin, who said he needed one ounce of gold to pay his ransom to the king. The ring weighed exactly one ounce, so Caisin got his freedom.

St Finnian (Richard King, *Capuchin Annual*)

The saint eventually reached Clonard in Co. Meath, where he settled. One day his pupil Senach realised how emaciated he was, his ribs showing through his clothes. Then he saw a worm coming out of his side, caused by the cold iron girdle he wore around him as a mortification for his body, and which cut into his very bone. His daily diet was a piece of barley bread and a glass of water. Only on Sundays and on Holy Days did he have a piece of broiled salmon and a full cup of mead or ale, as well as the piece of barley bread. He used to sleep neither on down nor flock, so that his side was on the bare earth and a stone served as a pillow.

Finnian's monastic school at Clonard became so important that he became known as 'tutor of the Saints of Ireland'. He himself is likely to have been the author of the oldest Irish penitential, the *Penitential of Vinnianus*. He died between 549 and 552. In time Clonard came to lead a league of Leinster monastic churches and its school attracted many of the foremost scholars of the country.

The ruins were swept away in the nineteenth century and the only surviving relic is a fine fifteenth-century font, with a carving of Finnian and other saints, now preserved in the Church of Ireland parish church which stands on part of the historic site.

Church ruins at Terryglass, Co. Tipperary

13 December

COLM [COLMAN MOCCU CREMTHANNAIN, COLUM]
of Terryglass, Co. Tipperary

St Colm (Richard King, *Capuchin Annual*)

Colm was a disciple of Colman Cule of Clonkeen and, later, one of Finnian's at Clonard. While he was at Clonard it was the job of Senan, who became Finnian's successor, to supervise the seminarians and to report to Finnian on what they were doing.

One day Senan told Finnian that one of them was kneeling in prayer, with his hands stretched out to heaven and so totally oblivious of all about him that birds came and lighted on his shoulders.

'That's the one,' said Finnian, 'who will give me the Last Rites.' This was Colm.

Colm became first abbot of Clonenagh, then went to other places and finally came from Inishcaltra to found Terryglass, which, under his rule, became a most celebrated centre of religion and learning. Columba was a visitor there. Colm is included as one of the 'Twelve Apostles of Ireland'.

Colm died in 549. Terryglass was associated with Tallaght and Clonenagh in the *Céile Dé* reform movement. All that remains are sparse ruins which are shamefully neglected.

114

19 December

SAFAN [SAMHTHANN]
of Clonbroney, Co. Longford

St Patrick is said to have given the veil to 'the two Emers', sisters of Guasacht, whom he put in charge of the church at Clonbroney in Co. Longford. Fuinech was the founder and first abbess, but Safan became the most famous abbess. She seems to have been very much a no-nonsense woman, as two ripostes made by her indicate. On one occasion a monk asked her what was the best position in which to pray. Her reply was that prayer should be made in every position. Another monk proposed to give up his studies in order to have more time for prayer but she pointed out that he would never be able to concentrate properly if he gave up studying. She died in 739.

22 December

EMIN [ÉIMHÍN, EVIN]
of Monasterevan, Co. Kildare

Emin was one of the six sons of Eoghan mac Murchad of the royal house of Munster. All six were founders of monasteries: Diarmaid at Kilmacowen, Co. Sligo; Cormac at Inishmaine, Co. Mayo; Becan at Kilpeacon, Co. Limerick; Culan at Glenkeen, Co. Tipperary, and Boedan at Kilboedain, Co. Antrim. Emin brought monks from his home-place and built his monastery at Monasterevan. He died in 689 and is buried there.

26 December

COMMAN [COMÁN]
of Roscommon, Co. Roscommon

Comman was a disciple of Finnian of Clonard and founded the monastery at Roscommon as abbot and bishop. He died in 549. No trace of the monastery remains today.

FURTHER READING

BIELER, L., *Ireland, Harbinger of the Middle Ages*, London, 1963.

DE PAOR, L. AND M., *Early Christian Ireland*, London, 1958.

DILLON, M., *Early Irish Literature*, Chicago, 1948.

HENRY, F., *Irish Art in the Early Christian Period*, London, 1965.

HUGHES, K., *The Church in Early Irish Society*, London, 1966.
   Early Christian Ireland: Introduction to the Sources, London, 1972.

HUGHES, K. AND HAMLIN, A., *The Modern Traveller to the Early Irish Church*,
   London, 1977.

LEASK, H.G., *Irish Churches and Monastic Buildings*, Dundalk, 1955.

MURPHY, G., *Early Irish Lyrics*, Oxford, 1956.

RYAN, M. (ED.), *Ireland and Insular Art A.D. 500–1200*, Dublin, 1987.

INDEX OF SAINTS' NAMES

Abban: Mar. 16; Aug. 24; Oct. 27
Acobhran: Jan. 28
ADHAMHNÁN: Sept. 23
ADOMNAN: Sept. 23
ADROCHTA*: Aug 11
Aedamar*: Jan. 18
AEDH: Nov. 10
Aedh: July 8
Aedhach: Apr. 9
AENGUS: Mar. 11; Sept. 3
Aghna*: May 18, 22
AGLENN*: Mar. 6
Aibhen: May 24
Aiffen: June 3
AIGLEND*: Mar. 6
AILBE: Sept. 12
Ailbe: Jan. 30
AILBHE: Sept. 12
Ailbhe: Sept. 10, 13; Dec. 29
Aileran: Dec. 29
Ailill: Jan. 13
Ailioll: July 1; Sept. 22
Ailithir: May 12
Ailltin*: Nov. 1
Ainbithen*: Jan. 2
Ainchi: Sept. 19
Ainmire: June 10; Sept. 15; Nov. 2
Aireid: Aug. 26
Airendan: Jan. 5
Aireran: May 7; Aug. 11
Airine: Nov. 30
Airmeadhach: Jan. 1
Airmne: Sept. 30
Aitche*: Jan. 15
Aithmet: Feb. 2
ALBY: Sept. 12
Alten: Jan. 11
Amphadan: Jan. 11

Ana*: Jan. 18
Annichad: Jan. 30
AODH: Nov. 10
Aodh: Jan. 4, 25; Feb. 7, 16; Apr. 7, 11;
  May 4, 10; June 27; July 10; Aug. 15,
  31; Sept. 22; Oct. 6, 29; Nov. 1
AODHÁN: Jan. 31
Aodhán: Jan. 1; Feb. 12; Mar. 16, 20,
  29; Apr. 1, 8; June 2, 17; July 19;
  Aug. 3, 7, 27, 31; Sept. 4, 20; Oct. 9,
  20; Nov. 6, 21; Dec. 25
Aodhnait*: Nov. 9
Aoldobhar: Nov. 19
Aonghus: Jan. 20; Feb. 16, 18; Nov. 17
ASSAN: Apr. 27
ASSICUS: Apr. 27
Athracht*: Feb. 9
ATHRACHTA*: Aug. 11
ATTRACTA*: Aug. 11

Baedan: Dec. 13
Baethin: June 9
Bain: Apr. 27
BAIRRE: Sept. 25
Baitan: Mar. 1
Baithen: June 18
Baithin: Jan. 9; Feb 19
Banbhan: Nov. 26
Banbhnat*: July 23
Baoithin: Jan. 19; May 22; Oct. 6
Baothghalach: Oct. 5
Barr: Aug. 22
Barran*: Aug. 9
BARRFHIONN: May 21
Barrfin: Sept. 22
Barrfionn: Nov. 8
BARRIND: May 21
BARUIN: May 21

Beacán: Feb. 26; Mar. 17; Apr. 5, 26;
  May 26; Aug. 17
Beaccán: Apr. 16
Beandan: Jan. 11
BEANNAN: Nov. 9
Bearach: Feb. 15; Apr. 21; June 10
Bearchán: May 7, 24; June 5; Nov. 24;
  Dec. 4
Bearnasca: May 12
Beatan: Jan. 14
Becan: Aug. 8
Becga*: Feb. 10
Bega: Sept. 6
BENEN: Nov. 9
BENIGNUS: Nov. 9
Beoan: Oct. 26
BEOC: Jan. 1
Beodan: Mar. 23
Beodh: Mar. 8
BEOG: Jan. 1
Beoghan: July 27
Beoghna: Aug. 22
BERCHAN: Oct. 12
Berchan: Aug. 4
Bhauch: Jan. 20
Bicsha*: June 28
Bigseach: Oct. 4
Bláth: Jan. 19
Bláth*: Jan. 29
Blathmac: Jan. 19
BLINNE*: July 6
Boga: Jan. 22
Boithin: Jan. 12
BOLCAN: Feb. 20
Bran: May 18
BRANDAN: May 16
Brandubh: June 3
Breaccan: Apr. 29; Dec. 6

119

Breacnat: July 3
Breague: June 4
Breannain: Jan. 9; May 8; July 27;
  Nov. 1, 29; Dec. 1, 8, 13
Breasal: May 18
Brecan: July 16; Aug. 9
BRENANN: May 16
BRENDAN: May 16
Brian: Apr. 23
BRÍD*: Feb. 1
BRIDGET*: Feb. 1
Brigh*: Jan. 7
BRIGHID*: Feb. 1
Brighid*: Mar. 6, 9; May 21; Aug. 12;
  Sept. 30
Brighis*: Jan. 21
BRIGID*: Feb. 1
Brigid*: Mar. 6
Brioch: May 1
Brocan: Jan. 1; June 27
Broccaidh: July 9
Broccan: July 8
Brogan: Apr. 9; Aug. 14
Bron: June 8
BRONACH*: Apr. 2
Bruinseach*: May 29
Buadan: July 22
Buadhan: Jan. 24
BUIN: Dec. 7
BUITE: Dec. 7
Buite: July 22
BUITHIN: Dec. 7

CAEMAN: Sept. 3
CAEMHAN: Sept. 3
Caemhan: June 6
Caencomhrac: July 23; Sept. 6
CAIMIN: Mar. 24
Caimin: Mar. 24
CAINNEACH: Oct. 11
Cairbre: Mar. 6; May 3; Nov. 11
Caireach*: Feb. 9
Cairetan: Mar. 7
Cairneach: Mar. 28
Caisin: Mar. 1
Camhan: Mar. 13

CAMIN: Mar. 24
CANICE: Oct. 11
Canneire*: Jan. 28
Caoide: Oct. 25
Caoilfhionn*: Feb. 3
Caoimgell: Sept. 19
Caoimhe*: Nov. 1, 2
Caoimhghell*: July 7
CAOIMHGHIN: June 3
Caoimhghin: May 11; Oct. 16
CAOIMHÍN: June 3
Caoimhseac*: Nov. 30
Caoinnete: Apr. 24
Caol*: Oct. 26
Caolán: June 19, 30; July 25, 29;
  Sept. 25; Oct. 29
Caomhán: Feb. 14, 22; Mar. 14, 18;
  Apr. 28; June 7, 12; Aug. 14;
  Sept. 14, 16; Oct. 16; Nov. 3; Dec. 18
Caomhsa*: Feb. 25
Caoncomhrac: June 29
Caorlan: Mar. 24
Caornan: Apr. 28
Carman: July 20
Carreall: July 13
CÁRTHACH: May 14
Cárthach: Mar. 5, 26
CARTHAGE: May 14
Cas: Apr. 26
CASSAN: Mar. 28
Cassan: June 4, 20
Cathabh: July 1
Cathal: Mar. 8; May 10
CATHBAD: Apr. 6
Cathcan: Mar. 20
CEALLACH: May 1
Ceallach: Jan. 23; Apr. 1, 7; May 13;
  July 18; Oct. 7
Ceallachan: Apr. 22; Sept. 24
Ceallan: May 1
Ceannfhealadh: Apr. 8
Céile Chríost: Mar. 3
Ceir: May 19
Celba: Aug. 21
Cellach: Aug. 20
Cera*: Feb. 8; Sept. 9

Cianán: Nov. 24, 29
Ciannait*: Mar. 23
Ciar: Oct. 16
Ciar*: Jan. 5; Oct. 13
CIARÁN: Mar. 5; Sept. 9
Ciarán: Jan. 5, 9; Feb. 4, 24; Mar. 8;
  Apr. 30; May 19; June 14; July 19;
  Aug. 9; Sept. 29; Oct. 8; Nov. 10
Ciarnan: Jan. 31
Cillene: Mar. 3
Cillian: Jan. 3, 8, 16; Mar. 3, 12, 26;
  Apr. 14, 19; May 27; July 3, 8;
  Aug. 7, 31; Oct. 22, 23; Dec. 28
Cillin: Apr. 12; June 27
Cinne*: Feb. 1
CLÁRAINECH: Oct. 12
Clothra*: Oct. 1
Coalchu: Sept. 24
Cobhran: Aug. 2
Cobhthach: July 30
Cobuir: July 30
Cocca: June 6, 29
Coghnat*: Feb. 11
Coibhdeanach: Nov. 26
Coine*: Apr. 4
Coinneach: Jan. 23, 31
Coireall: June 13
Coirpre: May 31
Colchu: Feb. 20
COLM: June 9; Dec. 13
Colm: Feb. 6; Mar. 1; May 15; June 4;
  Aug. 1; Sept. 2, 6, 22, 29; Oct. 1, 14,
  16; Nov. 8; Dec. 11
Colma*: Jan. 22
COLMAN: Feb. 3, 18, 21; June 7;
  Oct. 16; Nov. 25; Dec. 13
Colman: Jan. 1, 13, 22; Feb. 2, 7, 8, 9,
  14, 20; Mar. 10, 30, 31; Apr. 4, 9, 14;
  May 2, 6, 9, 15, 18, 20, 21, 24, 26;
  June 1, 2, 4, 6, 15, 16, 17, 18, 19, 26;
  July 8, 11, 12, 14, 19, 25, 31; Aug. 5,
  8, 9, 15, 18; Sept. 3, 6, 11, 12, 16, 22,
  25, 26, 29, 30; Oct. 1, 4, 6, 7, 13, 15,
  18, 19, 20, 24, 27, 28, 29, 30, 31;
  Nov. 1, 5, 7, 14, 21; Dec. 3, 5, 7, 10,
  12, 14, 15, 18, 23, 27

COLMCILLE: June 9
Colmoc: May 4
COLUM: Dec. 13
COLUMBA: June 9
Columban: Nov. 20
Comach*: May 27
COMÁN: Dec. 26
Comán: Mar. 18; Apr. 3; May 8, 15, 23;
    July 29; Oct. 31; Nov. 10, 21
COMGAL: May 10
COMGHAN: Feb. 27
COMHDAN: Feb. 27
COMHGALL: May 10
Comhghall: July 24, 28; Aug. 26;
    Sept. 4, 29; Oct. 7
Comhghan: Oct. 13
Commaigh*: Dec. 19
Commain: May 29
COMMAN: Dec. 26
Comman: July 15
Comnat*: Sept. 23
Comnatan*: Jan. 1
Conac*: Oct. 25
Conainne*: Mar. 8
Conall: Mar. 2, 3, 18; Apr. 2; May 12,
    22; June 2; Sept. 9
Conán: Jan. 12; Feb. 13; Mar. 8, 20;
    Apr. 26; July 1; Aug. 16
Conchenn*: Mar. 13
Condmach: July 9
Conmael: Sept. 11
Conna: Apr. 12; Sept. 30
Conna*: Mar. 3
Connait: Nov. 15
Connal: May 20
Connla: May 10; Dec. 30
Connlaed: May 3
Conodhar: Nov. 3
Conuan: June 29
Corcan: Jan. 7
Corcran: Oct. 8
Cormac: Jan. 7; Feb. 17; Mar. 26;
    June 21, 24; Aug. 17; Sept. 14;
    Oct. 15; Dec. 13, 14
Criomhthann: May 23
Criotan: Sept. 16

Critan: May 17
Croine: Jan. 27
Croine*: July 7
CRONAN: Feb. 10; Apr. 28
Cronan: Jan. 7, 20, 29, 30; Feb. 9, 12,
    20, 21, 25, 26; Mar. 8, 30; Apr. 6, 26;
    May 4; June 1, 12, 22; July 18, 24;
    Aug. 7, 30; Oct. 19, 28; Nov. 1, 6, 11;
    Dec. 15
Crone: Jan. 1
Cruimine: June 28
Cruinmael: June 22
Crunmaol: Dec. 17
Cuac*: Jan. 8
Cuach*: Apr. 29
Cuachnat*: Feb. 13
Cuan: Jan. 1; Mar. 2; July 10;
    Oct. 15, 29
Cuanan: Feb. 3
Cuanghas: Mar. 13
Cuann: Apr. 10
Cuanna: Feb. 4
Cuanna*: Feb. 3
Cuannan: Apr. 3
Cuimín: Jan. 12; Feb. 12, 24;
    May 19, 21; June 1; July 1, 29;
    Aug. 10, 14, 22; Sept. 1, 4, 17;
    Nov. 12, 30; Dec. 2, 18, 24
Cuintoc: May 27
Cuirbhin: July 20
Cuircne: Jan. 7
Cummainn*: May 28
Cunera*: June 12
Curcach*: July 21; Aug. 8
Curnan: Jan. 6

DABEOC: Jan. 1
Dachonna: May 15
Dachua: Aug. 10
Dadhnan: Apr. 11
Dagan: Sept. 13
DAIGH: Aug. 18
DAIRBHILE*: Aug. 3
DAIRCHELL: June 17
Daire*: Aug. 8
Dalbhac: Oct. 23

Dallan: Dec. 14
Dalua: Jan. 7
Damhan: Feb. 12
Damhnait*: May 15
DAMHNAT: June 13
DAMNAT: June 13
DARERCA*: July 6
Darerca*: Mar. 22
Darluaghach*: Feb. 1
Dartine*: July 3
DAVNET: June 13
DÉAGLÁN: July 24
DECLAN: July 24
DEGA: Aug. 18
DEIRDRE*: Jan. 15
Derbhile*: May 24; Oct. 26
DERIVLA*: Aug. 3
Derlugha*: Feb. 10
DERMOT: Jan. 10
DERVILL*: Aug. 3
DERVILLA*: Aug. 3
Deuraid: Jan. 13
DIARMAID: Jan. 10
Diarmaid: Jan. 6, 16; Apr. 24; June 21;
    July 8; Sept. 28; Oct. 12; Dec. 20
DICHU: Apr. 29
Dighde*: Apr. 25
DIMA: Jan. 6
Diman: Jan. 10
DIMMA: Jan. 6
Dinertach: Oct. 9
Diochuill: Mar. 15
DIOMA: Jan. 6
Dioman: June 27
Dioraid: July 27
DOMAINGERT: Jan. 6
Domangan: Apr. 29
Domhangart: Mar. 24
Domhnall: Apr. 17
Dónal: Apr. 26; Sept. 11
Donnán: Jan. 7; Apr. 17, 29; Aug. 11
Donnchadh: May 25; Oct. 22
Donoc: Feb. 13
Drostan: July 11
Dubhan: Feb. 11; Nov. 11
Dubhthach: Oct. 7

Duileach: Nov. 17
Duinseach*: Aug. 5
Duthac: June 26
Duthracht: May 16

Eabhnat*: Jan. 31
Éadaoin*: July 5
Eanan: Jan. 30; Mar. 1, 25; Apr. 29;
   Aug. 19; Sept. 2; Dec. 29
ÉANNA: Mar. 21
Éanna: Dec. 31
EARC: Nov. 2
Earnán: Jan. 11, 17; May 16; Aug. 17;
   Oct. 26, 27
Eghneach: Apr. 24
Eglionna*: Jan. 21
Egol: June 1
Eimher: Aug. 13
ÉIMHÍN: Dec. 22
Éimhín: Jan. 7; Dec. 18
EINNE: Mar. 21
Eirnín: Jan. 26; Feb. 23, 28; Apr. 12;
   May 12, 31; June 4, 28; July 1, 13;
   Aug. 5, 18; Nov. 12, 13; Dec. 14, 23
EITHNE*: Jan. 11
Eithne*: Feb. 25, 26; Mar. 2; July 6
EMIN: Dec. 22
Emin: Apr. 12
Enan: Sept. 18
ENDA: Mar. 21
Eoain: Sept. 18
Eochaid: Jan. 1, 25, 29; Apr. 17
EOGHAN: Aug. 23
Eoghan: Mar. 3, 15; Apr. 18; May 28,
   31; June 11; Oct. 16; Dec. 20
Eolog: Sept. 5
ERC: Nov. 2
Erc: July 13
Ercnac*: Jan. 8
Ercnat*: Oct. 30
Ermen*: Feb. 13
Ernab: Jan. 1
Ernan: Aug. 19
Escon: Nov. 19
Etchen: Feb. 11
Ethian: May 27

ETHNEA*: Jan. 11
EUGENE: Aug. 23
EUNAN: Sept. 23
EVIN: Dec. 22

FACHTNA: Aug. 14
Fachtna: Jan. 19; Feb. 12; Mar. 3;
   July 14, 24; Aug. 24
Faelan: Sept. 5
Failbhe: Jan. 11; Feb. 8; Mar. 10, 22;
   Apr. 8, 16; June 19, 30; July 11, 18,
   20; Aug. 1; Sept. 1, 4
Faile*: Mar. 3
Fainche*: Jan. 1, 21
Faithleann: June 4
Faolán: Jan. 9; Mar. 31; Apr. 3; May 5,
   28; June 6, 20, 23; Aug. 24, 26;
   Sept. 30; Oct. 12, 19, 31; Nov. 5
Faolchu: July 20
Faoldobhair: June 29
Faoltiarna: Mar. 17
Fearfhuighill: Mar. 10
Fearghus: Jan. 20; Feb. 15; Mar. 23, 29,
   30; Apr. 27; July 5, 19; Sept. 8, 10;
   Nov. 10
Feargna: Mar. 2
FECHIN: Jan. 20
FEDELMIA*: Jan. 11
Fedhbar*: Nov. 6
FEICHÍN: Jan. 20
Feichín: Feb. 19, 22; Aug. 2; Dec. 28
Feidelm*: Dec. 9
FEIDLIMIDH: Aug. 9
Feidlimidh: Aug. 3, 28; Oct. 30;
   Dec. 20, 23
FELIM: Aug. 9
Felmac: Mar. 16
Fema*: Sept. 17
Fethaidh: Mar. 31
FIACC: Oct. 12
FIACH: Oct. 12
Fiacha: Dec. 27
Fiachna: Apr. 29
FIACHRA: Feb. 8
Fiachra: May 2; July 25; Aug. 30;
   Sept. 28

FIACRE: Feb. 8
Fiadhar: July 7
Fiadhnait*: Nov. 29
Fianait*: Jan. 4
FIDELMA*: Jan. 11
FINAN: Apr. 7
FINBAR: Sept. 25
Finchan: June 4
Finche*: Jan. 25
FINCHU: Nov. 25
FINDCHU: Nov. 25
Findchu: Mar. 11
Findlugh: May 11; June 5
Findsech*: Oct. 13
Finghin: Feb. 5
FINIAN: Dec. 12
Finnan: Feb. 16; Aug. 17
Finnech*: Feb. 2; June 25
Finnen: Aug. 29
Finnia*: Jan. 9; Feb. 11
FINNIAN: Feb. 23; Sept. 10; Dec. 12
Finnian: Mar. 2; May 17; Sept. 27
FINNIO: Dec. 12
FINTAN: Feb. 17; Oct. 21
Fintan: Mar. 26
Fiodhmuine: May 16
Fionán: Jan. 8; Feb. 12, 13; Mar. 16;
   Oct. 4; Nov. 25; Dec. 8
Fionbarr: July 4
Fionnan: Dec. 29
FIONNBARR: Sept. 25
Fionnbharr: May 21; July 25; Sept. 9, 10
FIONNCHU: Nov. 25
Fionnlugh: Jan. 3
FIONNTÁN: Oct. 21
Fionntán: Jan. 1, 3; Feb. 7, 21; Mar. 27;
   May 11; July 13, 18; Sept. 8, 19;
   Oct. 1, 9, 10, 20; Nov. 7, 9, 16;
   Dec. 14
Flann: Jan. 14, 21; Apr. 20, 24; July 6,
   17; Dec. 15, 21
Flannán: Mar. 14; Aug. 28; Nov. 5;
   Dec. 12, 18
Fleid*: Sept. 12
Foelan: Jan. 12
Foillan: July 23

122

Forannan: Apr. 30
Forodhran: June 18; July 28
Fortchern: Oct. 11
Forthach: Oct. 5
Fridolin: Mar. 4
Froechan: Nov. 20
Fulartach: Mar. 29

Gall: Oct. 16
Gallus: Apr. 4
Galma*: Oct. 15
Garbhán: Mar. 26; Apr. 17; May 14;
   July 9; Nov. 21
Gerald: Mar. 13
Gilda Nachal-Beo: Mar. 31
Giobhnenn: May 23
Giolla Chríost: June 12
Giolla Mac Leig: Mar. 27
GOBAN: Dec. 6
Goban: June 20
GOBBAN: Dec. 6
Gobban: Mar. 17; Apr. 1
Gobhan: Mar. 26
GOBNAT*: Feb. 11
Gorman: Oct. 25
Gormgall: Aug. 5
Greallan: July 13
Grellan: Sept. 17
Guaire: Jan. 9, 22, 25; June 22; July 27
Guasacht: Jan. 24
Guibseach: June 20

HUGH: Nov. 10

Iarfhlaith: Dec. 26
IARLAITH: June 6
Iarnoc: July 31
IBAR: Apr. 23
IBHAR: Apr. 23
ÍDE*: Jan. 15
Indreachtach: Apr. 26
Inna: Jan. 7
Iomhar: Aug. 12
ITA*: Jan. 15
ITE*: Jan. 15
IVAR: Apr. 23

JARLATH: June 6

KELLACH: May 1
KEVIN: June 3
KIERAN: Mar. 5; Sept. 9

LACHTAN: Mar. 19
LAICHTAN: Mar. 19
Laichtein: June 26
LAICHTIN: Mar. 19
Laidcenn: Jan. 12
Laidchenn: May 20
Laidgenn: Nov. 28
LAISRE: Sept. 12
Laisre: May 7
Laisre*: May 11, 14
LAISREN: Apr. 18; Aug. 12; Sept. 12
Lalloc: Feb. 6
Lappan: Mar. 26
Lasair*: Jan. 22; Aug. 20
Lasairian: Aug. 13; Sept. 16; Oct. 25;
   Dec. 26
LASERIAN: Apr. 18
LASREN: Sept. 12
Lassair: Mar. 29; Sept. 15
Lassair*: Jan. 6; Mar. 17; Apr. 18
Lean: June 5
Leccan: Apr. 27
Liadhain*: Aug. 11
Liadhnan: Feb. 5; Oct. 2
Liamhan*: Mar. 22
Liban: June 1
Lioban*: Dec. 18
Liobran: Mar. 11
Liucan: July 28
Loarn: Aug. 30; Sept. 11
Loban: June 5
Lochaidh: Jan. 2
LOCHAN: Sept. 25
Lochan: Jan. 16; Dec. 31
Lochein: Jan. 12
Lochen: June 12
Loigteach: Oct. 1
LOMÁN: Oct. 11
Lomán: Feb. 4, 7, 17
LOMMAN: Oct. 11

Lon: June 24
Lonán: Feb. 7; June 6; July 11; Aug. 2;
   Oct. 18, 24; Nov. 1, 12
Lorcán: Nov. 13, 14
LUA: Aug. 4
Lua: June 4
Luaithren*: June 8
Luan: May 12; June 25; July 21
Lucan: Jan. 23, 27; Aug. 12
Luchan: Apr. 22
Lughaid: Mar. 24; July 1
Lughaidh: Jan. 31; Feb. 12; Mar. 9;
   Apr. 17; June 25; Aug. 6; Sept. 30;
   Oct. 6; Nov. 2
Lughaire: May 11
Lughan: Aug. 16
Lugna: Apr. 25
LUGUID: Aug. 4
Luicridh: Apr. 29
Luighseach: May 22
Luightighearna: Apr. 28
Luit*: July 27
Luith*: Apr. 30
Luithrenn*: May 1
Lurach: Feb. 17
Luran: June 2; Oct. 29

Mac Caille: Apr. 25
MAC CARTAN: Mar. 24
MAC CARTHENN: Mar. 24
MAC NISSI: Sept. 3
Maccoige: Dec. 3
Macha*: Mar. 6
Machan: Sept. 28
Maedhbh*: Nov. 22
Maeiosa: Jan. 16
Maelbhrighde: Jan. 30
Maelcoisne: Sept. 8
Maelcorghais: Mar. 12
Maelcritiog: Oct. 8
Maeldoid: June 29
Maelfhionnain: Feb. 6
MAELRUAIN: July 7
Maelrubha: Apr. 21
Maeltolaigh: Sept. 13
Maeltuile: May 29

MAHEE: June 23
Maighnenn: Dec. 18
MAINCHÍN: Jan. 2
Mainchín: Jan. 13; Feb. 14; Mar. 23;
    May 1; Oct. 21; Nov. 12;
    Dec. 2, 4, 29
Mainne: Sept. 2
MALACHY: Nov. 2
Malchus: Aug. 10
Malcoisne: Aug. 16
Maloc: Apr. 16
MANCHAN: Jan. 2
Mantan: Mar. 2, 24
M'AODHOG: Jan. 31
Maodhog: Apr. 11
Maoilanfhaidh: Jan. 31
Maolam: Jan. 4
Maolan: Dec. 25
Maolcethair: May 14
Maoldobharchon: Feb. 19
Maolmaedhog: Nov. 3
Maolmhuire: July 3; Dec. 24
Maolochtraigh: Apr. 20
Maolodhran: Jan. 10; May 31; July 16;
    Nov. 11; Dec. 2
MAOLRUAIN: July 7
Maoltuile: July 30
Maonacan: Feb. 7
Maonach: Oct. 17
Meadhran: June 8
Meallán: Feb. 7; Dec. 6
Meattan*: Mar. 7
Mella*: Mar. 9, 19, 31
Meltog: Dec. 11
Meno: Sept. 18
Miacca*: Aug. 1
Mianach: Apr. 23; Aug. 11
Mianach*: July 18
Mica*: Jan. 17
Michen: Aug. 25
MIDA*: Jan. 15
Miodhnat: Aug. 4; Nov. 18
Miolan: Apr. 16
MIONNAN: Nov. 9
MOBEOC: Jan. 1
Mobheoc: Dec. 16

MO-BHI: Oct. 12
Mobhi: Oct. 2
MO-BI: Oct. 12
Mocadoc: Feb. 24
Mocellach: Mar. 7
Mochaemhoch: Mar. 13
Mochaemoc: Apr. 13
MOCHAOI: June 23
Mocheallach: Mar. 26
Mochiarog: May 7
Mocholla: Mar. 23
MO-CHOLMOG: June 7
Mochonna: Jan. 13; Mar. 8, 27;
    May 13, 19; June 7
Mochritoch: May 11
MOCHTA: Aug. 19
Mochta: Mar. 26
MO-CHUA: Feb. 10
Mochua: Mar. 3, 19; May 4; June 3;
    Aug. 6; Dec. 24
MO-CHUDA: May 14
Mochumma: Jan. 4, 5
Modhomhnoc: Feb. 13; May 18
Modichu: Jan. 7
Modimog: Dec. 10
MO-ECA: Jan. 20
MOEDOC: Jan. 31
Moelan: May 27
Moeldod: May 13
MO-FHECA: Jan. 20
MO-FHINNU: Oct. 21
Mogenog: Dec. 26
Moghaidh: Sept. 20
Moghain*: Dec. 15
MOGUE: Jan. 31
Moinenn: Mar. 1
Moinne: May 21
Molacca: Jan. 7; Aug. 7
MO-LACHTOG: Mar. 19
MO-LAISSE: Apr. 18; Aug. 12; Sept. 12
Moliba: Jan. 8; Dec. 26
MO-LING: June 17
Molioba: Aug. 5
Moliobba: Feb. 18
Molotha*: Sept. 2
MOLUA: Aug. 4

Molua: May 11
Mo-Maedoc: Aug. 13
Momhanna*: Mar. 21
Monessa: Mar. 15
MONINNA*: July 6
MONINNE*: July 6
Moninne: Apr. 18
Moninne*: May 23; June 3
Monoa*: Jan. 16
MO-RI: Aug. 1
Mosacro: Mar. 3
Mo-Siollach: July 13
Mothrenoch: Aug. 20
Mo-Ulloch: Mar. 20
Muadan: Aug. 30
Muadhnait*: Jan. 6
Muicin: Mar. 4
MUINCHIN: Jan. 2
MUIREADHACH: Aug. 13
Muireadhach: May 15; Dec. 28
Muiredheabhar: Nov. 3
Muirgin: Jan. 27
MULLIN: June 17
MULLING: June 17
MULROON: July 7
MUNCHIN: Jan. 2
MUNNU: Oct. 21
MURA: Mar. 12
Murgal: Sept. 30

NAAL: July 31
Naal: Jan. 27
NADAL: July 31
NADAN: July 31
NAEL: July 31
Nainnid: Nov. 13
Naomhan: Sept. 13
Nasan: July 12
NATALIS: July 31
Natchaoim: May 1
Nathi: Aug. 1, 9
Neachtan: Jan. 8; May 2
Neachtan*: Nov. 22
Neallan: Jan. 28
Neasan: Sept. 29; Dec. 1, 6
NEASSAN: July 25

124

Nem: May 3; June 19
Nemen: Sept. 1
Neslugh: Mar. 15
NESSAN: July 25
Nessan: Mar. 17
Niadh: June 5
Ninidh: Apr. 21
Ninnidh: Jan. 16; June 2
NOTAN: July 31
Nuada: Oct. 3
Nuadhan: Feb. 6

Oda: Feb. 27
Odharnait★: Nov. 13
ODHRÁN: Oct. 2
Odhrán: Feb. 18, 19; Mar. 6; May 8, 16;
    Aug. 18; Sept. 10; Oct. 26, 27
OENGUS: Mar. 11
Oisín: Feb. 17; May 1; July 19, 22
Olan: Sept. 5
OLCAN: Feb. 20
Olcan: July 4
Oliver: July 11
Ollan: Dec. 7
Onchu: Feb. 8; July 9, 14
ORAN: Oct. 2
Orthinis: Jan. 11
Osmana: Sept. 9
Osnat: Jan. 6
Osnat★: Nov. 10

PÁDRAIG: Mar. 17
PATRICK: Mar. 17
Proinnséas: Mar. 9

Ranait: Aug. 5
Riaghail: Sept. 17
Richeal: May 19
RIOCH: Aug. 1
RI-OG: Aug. 1
Riognach★: Dec. 18
Rodaighe: Dec. 16
Roibhne: Feb. 16
Roinne: Nov. 23
RONAN: Nov. 18

Ronan: Jan. 11, 13; Feb. 6, 9; Apr. 8,
    30; May 1, 21, 22; June 1; Dec. 23
Ronana: Aug. 18
RUADHÁN: Apr. 15
RUAN: Apr. 15
Rufin: Apr. 22
Ruidche★: Feb. 8
Ruisin: Apr. 7
Runach: July 23
Russen: Apr. 29

SAFAN: Dec. 19
Saighin: Jan. 21
SAMHTHANN: Dec. 19
Sanctan: May 9
Saodhbhar: June 26
Saorgus: May 30
Saran: Jan. 8, 13; Mar. 1; July 30;
    Aug. 1, 15; Sept. 21
SARBHILE★: July 6
Sarnat★: Apr. 15; May 3
Scannall: May 3
Sceallan: Sept. 1
Sciath: Jan. 1
Sciath★: Sept. 6
Scire★: Mar. 24
Scoithin: Jan. 2
Scoth★: July 16
Seachnall: Nov. 27
Séadna: Mar. 9, 10; June 16
SEANÁN: Mar. 8
Seanán: Mar. 1; Apr. 7, 9, 11, 26;
    May 5; June 2; July 10; Aug. 17;
    Sept. 4, 16, 25, 30; Oct. 4, 10; Dec. 5,
    18, 24
Sedrachor: Apr. 20
Segen: Sept. 10
Seighin: Aug. 24
SENA: Mar. 8
Senach: May 11; Dec. 10
Senan: Aug. 7
SENANUS: Mar. 8
Senchadh: Dec. 17
Sensa: July 30
Serbhile★: Sept. 4
Sessen: Aug. 31

Siadhal: Jan. 31; Feb. 12; Mar. 8
Sillan: Jan. 31; June 3
Silvester: Mar. 10
Sinach: July 16; Sept. 28
Sinche★: Aug. 22
SINCHEALL: Mar. 26
SINCHELL: Mar. 26
Sineach★: Nov. 9
Sinech★: Oct. 5
Sinel: Nov. 11
Sinell: Jan. 12
Siollan: Feb. 10, 28; Mar. 28; May 4,
    17, 24; July 21; Aug. 25; Sept. 7, 11;
    Dec. 21
Siollan★: Oct. 10
Sionach: Aug. 21
Sionnach: Apr. 20
Siubsech★: Jan. 9
Slebine: Mar. 2
Sobhartan: Apr. 20
Sodealbh★: Mar. 29
Stellan: May 24; June 1
Suairleach: Apr. 23
Suibhne: Jan. 11, 19; Apr. 28;
    June 21, 22; Oct. 28
Suirleach: Mar. 21, 27

Tadg: July 8; Aug. 7
Tadhg: Oct. 24
Taimhthionna★: Oct. 29
Talla★: Aug. 11
Talmach: Feb. 25, 26; Mar. 14
TASSACH: Apr. 14
Tearnoch: Oct. 3
Teca★: Oct. 18
Tecla★: Sept. 23
Teimhen: Aug. 17
Telle: June 25
Tenan: July 16
Tenna: July 21
Ternoc: Jan. 8; July 2
Tiarnach: Mar. 17; May 13; July 7;
    Nov. 4
Tiarnán: Apr. 8
Tigearnach: Apr. 5
TIGERNEACH: Apr. 4

TIGHERNACH: Apr. 4
TIHERNACH: Apr. 4
Tiobrat: Dec. 27
Tiu*: June 24
Tobrea: Jan. 1
Toccomhracht: June 11
Toit: Sept. 7
Tola: Mar. 30
Toma: Apr. 22

Toman: Jan. 10; Mar. 18; July 26;
  Nov. 30
Torannan: June 12
Torbach: July 16
Trea*: Aug. 3
Trian: Mar. 22
Tua: Dec. 22
Tuan: Apr. 1
Tuilelath*: Jan. 6, 10

Uinchin: Aug. 21
ULTAN: Sept. 4
Ultan: Jan. 17; Mar. 14; Apr. 4, 16, 27;
  May 1, 24; July 1, 3, 5, 10, 12;
  Aug. 9; Sept. 7; Nov. 22; Dec. 22
Usaille: Aug. 27

SELECT INDEX OF PLACE NAMES